MEDIA POLICY AND NATION BUILDING

About the Authors

V. S. Gupta, presently Professor at the Haryana Agricultural University, was awarded the UNDP Fellowship for training in Europe and was selected for the Journalist Fellowship Award for working in the area of Environment and Development.

He has contributed a large number of papers in seminars, conferences and academic journals in India and abroad. Some of the publications edited by him include : *Media and Development (1994)* with M. R. Dua and *Rural Press—Problems and Prospects (1995)* with Rajeshwar Dyal. His book, *Third Revolution in Indian Perspective : Contemporary Issues and Themes in Communication (1995)* has been very well received in India and abroad.

Prof. Gupta is associated with academic programmes in journalism and mass communication at the post-graduate level of several universities in the country. He represents the Asian Mass Communication Research and Information Centre (AMIC) Singapore, as its representative in India.

Vir Bala Aggarwal is on the faculty of the Department of Journalism and Mass Communication, Himachal Pradesh University, Shimla. She has contributed a number of research and popular papers to academic journals, seminars and conferences. She has been frequently writing on Media, Development and Women Issues. With Prof. Gupta, she has been associated with the Toyota Foundation Project for the translation of AMIC publications.

MEDIA POLICY AND NATION BUILDING

Select Issues and Themes

V. S. GUPTA
Professor
Haryana Agricultural University
Hisar

VIR BALA AGGARWAL
Assistant Professor
Department of Journalism and
Mass Communication,
Himachal Pradesh University
Shimla

CONCEPT PUBLISHING COMPANY, NEW DELHI-110 059

ISBN 81-7022-590-6

First Published 1996

Published and Printed by
Ashok Kumar Mittal
Concept Publishing Company
A/15-16, Commercial Block, Mohan Garden
New Delhi-110 059 (India)
Phones : 550 4042, 555 4042

PREFACE

The Ministry of Information and Broadcasting in 1994 brought out a Discussion Paper — Note on National Media Policy. Subsequently, it also developed and circulated a questionnaire for eliciting the opinion of cross section of people from all over the country. During the last two years Namedia Foundation and the Indian Chapter of the Asian Mass Communication Research and Information Centre organised seminars, dialogues and colloquium on the subject.

While the exercise to evolve a Media Policy at various levels is still to crystalise in firm conclusions and guidelines, we thought it fit to focus the debate on the role that Media Policy can play in, and the contribution it can make to the efforts of nation building. Equally important is to emphasise that fast changing media scenario in the country notwithstanding — it would still be relevant to come back to the basics—harnessing the potential of media for issues such as rural development, empowerment of women, distance education, environmental protection, etc. We also felt concerned that the emerging Information Society in India is creating problems of a different nature—the gap between the information rich and the information poor. The latest developments in policy making, which would naturally include the landmark judgement of the Supreme Court on establishing an autonomous statutory Public Broadcasting Authority, have come in for detailed discussion.

We hope that the book would serve the purpose of nation-wide debate on formulation of a Media Policy with Nation Building as its primary focus. We would feel amply rewarded, if in the process, the book provides an input and a reference point in the shaping of Media Policy in the country.

We owe a debt of deep gratitude to the chiefs of the two organisations — Mr. Vijay Menon, Secretary-General, Asian Mass Communication Research and Information Centre, Singapore and Dr. Heinz Bongartz, Resident Representative of the Friedric Ebert Stiftung in New Delhi, who provided us with a forum and opportunity of interacting with a large number of participants— academics, media persons and policy makers at various seminars; and their encouragement to academic publishing. Our two colleagues — D. C. Yadav and J. C. Malhotra have rendered valuable assistance at various stages of preparation of the manuscript and production of the book. We would also like to express our sincere appreciation to our publisher, Ashok Mittal, who as usual, put up with our uncertain schedule and deferred deadlines.

V. S. Gupta
Vir Bala Aggarwal

CONTENTS

LIST OF ABBREVIATIONS

AIR	All India Radio
AMIC	Asian Mass Communication Research and Information Centre
APIBD	Asian Pacific Institute of Broadcasting Development
ASCI	Advertising Standards Council of India
BBC	British Broadcasting Corporation
BES	Broadcasting Engineering Society
C-DOT	Centre for Development of Telematics
CNN	Cable News Network
COL	Commonwealth of Learning
CPA	Consumer Protection Act
DAB	Digital Audio Broadcasting
DPAP	Drought Prone Area Programme
DSC	Development Support Communication
ERNET	Education and Research in Network
FAO	Food and Agriculture Organisation
FES	Friedrich Ebert Stiftung
FFW	Food for Work
GDP	Gross Development Product
GNP	Gross National Product
HDI	Human Development Index
ICPD	International Conference on Population and Development
IGNOU	Indira Gandhi National Open University
INSAT	Indian National Satellite
IPDC	International Programme for Development Communication
IRDP	Integrated Rural Development Programme
ISRO	Indian Space Research Organisation
NIMME	National Institute of Multi-Media Education
NICNET	National Information Centre Network
NPG	National Performance Gap
SAC	Space Application Centre
SFDS	Small Farmers Development Agency
SITE	Satellite Instructional Television Experiment
TRYSEM	Training of Rural Youth for Self-Employment
UNDP	United Nations Development Programme
UNESCO	United Nations Educational Scientific and Cultural Organization

1

INTRODUCTION

The focal theme in Media Policy and Nation Building today is the potential and possibilities of the use of media structures, and their exploitation for the task of nation building. Whereas there has been exponential expansion and modernisation in media systems during the past decade, there is not as yet adequate policy frame and mechanism between media and nation building. Apart from its use as an agency for government propaganda, the government controlled electronic media has yet to emerge as an important policy instrument in the social, educational and development planning.

Apart from building human capital, other major elements of Nation Building have been generally spelt out in, *Communications Policy for National Development — A Comparative Perspective (1977)* : The progress of a nation depends first and foremost on the progress of its people. Unless it develops their spirit and human potentialities, it cannot develop much else... materially, economically, politically or culturally. Hence, their first task must be to build up their human capital. To put it in more human terms, that means improving the education, skills, and hopefulness, and thus the mental and physical health of their men, women and children. It further adds : To raise educational standards in developing countries requires the dissemination of knowledge on farming, industrial skills, health, nutrition and community development as well as provisions for mass education to overcome illiteracy. But in an attempt to accomplish in years what took centuries in developed countries, traditional educational methods appear inadequate. Mass media and scientific approaches seem to offer the greatest promise.

Throughout its history India has managed to survive and make social and economic progress without a major segment of its population being able to read or write. With rapidly growing sophistication, urbanisation and now enhanced opportunities because of economic liberalisation, illiteracy will prove to be a majốr bottleneck. Moreover, the complexities of modern living underscores the importance of basic essentials — literacy, civic consciousness, environmental protection, human rights awareness. Therefore, inspite of print media in regional languages having made rapid strides, in the planning of a media policy, audio visual media, radio and television will continue to be important. A large part of this book is devoted to contemporary issues concerning the print and electronic media.

A Preview of Chapters

The debate on Media Policy has been characterised by scepticism whether, in the first place — should India have a Media Policy? Should we have a Media Policy or would not generally accepted codes, norms and guidelines evolved by professional bodies, be more practicable to implement? At the same time veteran broadcaster Mehra Masani felt that lack of progress in organised broadcasting was due to the absence of Communication Policy. There have also been questions : When we have an Industrial Policy or when we could evolve even an Agricultural Policy, why not at least initiate a debate leading to the formulation of a Media Policy. It is hoped that as we go along, we have better perspective on a large number of issues involved.

As India gets on to the threshold of an Information Society, with a boom in satellite and cable television, introduction of cellular and paging services, India World on Internet, once again there are genuine apprehensions that these developments would result in accentuating the gap between the information rich and the information poor. At the same time there has also been a feeling that information technologies cannot do much to solve the most serious national problems, which in India's case were identified as poverty, education and regional politics. Even in industrialised countries there are doubts as to the efficacy of the newly emerging dispensation for the Third World nations. The questions which have been raised in this context include : Plagued by barriers of poverty, poor health, low life expectancy, illiteracy, little access to tertiary education, emerging countries must compete with advanced countries in a highly competitive global market place. What does Information Society mean to them? Can these Third World nations ever catch up?

It has, therefore, been stressed that while laying down Media Policy, the government and bureaucrats of the Information and Broadcasting Ministry are not swayed by a mind-set conditioned by newly emerging, dazzling spectrum of technologies like 61-television channels, information superhighways, etc.

The focus of the chapter, Media Policy and Nation Building, is on National Development, which would generally mean : mobilizing human potential through (a) access to material resources like good health, education, housing and food and (b) creation of a culture and environment that guarantees freedom, human rights and personal self-respect. In case of India, the nation building process has been identified around the creation of a realm of central values as embodied in the preamble of the constitution in the creation of a secular, socialist and democratic society and would entail removal of caste, religious, ethnic, regional inequalities, decentralized planning by involving local groups and leaders, detribalization of a large section of population, removal of inequalities and disparities in income, wealth and employment among groups, and curbing gender inequality. Among the factors determining nation building, Environmental Protection, Empowerment of Women, Consumer Protection, Educational Development and Rural Development have been discussed in detail. The issue of evolving 'Information and Communication Strategies' has been adequately addressed. Many development thinkers and agencies are becoming increasingly determined that people's needs and demands are more fully understood, and wherever appropriate, integrated into wider development context. But mere identification of information needs of scientists, policy makers and planners, extension workers, rural community groups and information/communication problems vis-a-vis rural development, has no meaning unless it is matched by the design and development of appropriate information and communication strategies.

Reducing Inequalities in Communication and Development

The main problem facing the country today, however, is not the lack of technologies and scientific discoveries needed for nation building, but converting these into production accomplishments and using them as an instrument of economic growth and social change. Unless we are able to reduce inequalities in communication and development, and the personnel engaged in development communication work — broadcasters, producers and writers are re-educated and made conscious of the needs and problems of the unprivileged, and positive gain shown in increased GNP is meaningless.

While formulating Media Policy, it will be essential to take note of what P. C. Joshi says in Sardar Patel Memorial Lectures 1985 : *Commu-*

nication and Nation Building–Perspective and Policy :

> Between the cultural and communication apparatus of the government and non-government agencies on the one hand and the policy-making and policy-implementing departments and agencies on the other hand, there seems to be not much communication nor integration and coordination. The ministries of the central and state governments engaged in nation building and development tasks seem to create neither any communication awareness apparatus within their own ministries nor do they make demands on the Ministry of Information and Broadcasting for information and communication support adequate to the needs of policy formulation or implementation. The Information and Broadcasting Ministry is far from playing the role of a true communicating link within the government and between the government and the people in nation-building activities. It utilises its wide network and substantial resources to a large extent for "entertainment" without integrating socially relevant and useful message in entertainment itself. The vast potential of entertainment as a carrier of relevant messages is being exploited by advertising agencies and not by development agencies. The mass media have had no significant role in making different sections of society plan-conscious nor have they evolved an integrated view of entertainment and non-entertainment needs.

Writing on the Role of Broadcasting in Social and Economic Development, Ithiel de Sola Pool says in the book, *Communication Policy for National Development — A Comparative Perspective* : Development broadcasting demands close coordination with the concerned government departments and other institutions responsible for implementation. It would be pointless, for instance, to promote a new seed variety if it is unavailable in the localities where it is to be used .... As a development agency, a broadcasting organization has the critical responsibility of activating the human potential of the country and its cultural development. This contribution to development can be provided not only by serious educational programmes but also by those whose primary aim is entertainment. Entertainment programming can present audiences with role models for new ways of life and can fulfil an informative role as well as, or even better than, programming which is more purposively informative.

Changing Values in Journalism

The concern over lowering ethical values in media has been shared. These sharp practices, by no means restricted to the Indian journalists, tend to erode the credibility of the profession as such. It has been suggested that a code of ethics needs to be formulated by professional bodies and mediamen which should be displayed in the reporter's room and on the newsdesk. The Note on the National Media Policy, issued as a Discussion Paper, by the Ministry of Information and Broadcasting, also points out that the press should repudiate the extension of any direct financial assistance or subsidy in the form of release of government advertisements, etc. that may ultimately dilute the freedom. The Note also wants that government must seriously consider withdrawing the facility of provision of residential accommodation, etc.

The encouragement of linguistic, sectarian and ethnic passions, working to the advantage of fissiparous tendencies, by regional language newspapers has also been noticed as against basics of nation building.

Electronic Media Policy

The impact of rapidly proliferating cable television on the minds of young students — kitsch and thrill syndrome, trivilising of even normal and straight forward programmes, had been widely reported in the press during the past two years. A study conducted by the Media Advocacy Group in 1994 established that parents were apprehensive about the impact which excessive vulgarity and violence was likely to have on children. The Study pointed out : Any effort to commercialise the medium at the cost of societal obligations should be avoided, particularly during prime time. It was suggested that whereas censorship may not work, a self-regulatory body of producers and owners of satellite channels may evolve mutually accepted guidelines and exercise some degree of control over the quality of programmes.

The Electronic Media Policy will have to incorporate essential elements of the Prasar Bharati Act (1990) and the Supreme Court Judgement, February 1995, which have been adequately discussed in the text. Notwithstanding the assurances of the government to set up an autonomous public broadcast authority 'fairly quickly' (March 1995); nothing concrete is on the anvil so far.

It also been observed that any discussion on electronic media policy tends to sideline the contribution and efficacy of radio, which has a noteworthy and illustrious record of public service broadcasting. Since television is being driven more and more by market forces and the objective of using it as a tool for development has been relegated to sideways, to underline the importance of radio for development is obvious. The urgency of public accountability of media, through national bodies constituted of professionals, public persons, activist groups and voluntary organisations, has been voiced for a long time, more so in the recent past. Some of the watchdog mechanisms and regulatory measures have already been in place, Press Council of India being the most well known; it is equally essential that Broadcasting Council, as envisaged in the Prasar Bharati Bill be constituted. The institution of Ombudsman by the *Times of India*, the Press Advisory Council and Monitoring Editors by *Asahi Shimbun*, one of Japan's largest newspapers, have been some of the instances, which have worked with varying degree of success.

One of the legitimate and widely recurring issues confronting the media analysts is : Deviation between Laws and Codes as Written and in Actual Practice. In this context, Venkateswaran (1993) points out :

> Complaints have ranged from grossly disproportionate use of broadcast time to present the ruling party's viewpoint to the near total exclusion of other view points, denial of access to those representing opposing, non-conformist or minority interests, blatant distortion of news to the government's advantage and so on — complaints which are not always amenable to judicial adjudication. The absence of an independent watchdog to which the aggrieved can turn, has only served to exacerbate the consequent feeling of helplessness engendered in the community. It is a measure of the frustration felt on this score that some public spirited citizens and institutions have begun approaching the courts to challenge the state monopoly over radio and television.

The Contribution of media to nation building would be immeasurably enhanced if certain steps, some of these articulated even before are initiated : Exclusive TV and Radio Channel for Increased Rural Programmes, Training Programmes for Rural Journalists, Constitution of a National Council for Mass Communication and a National Council for Listeners and Viewers and franchise stations for research institutions, academic bodies and universities.

We will do well to bear in mind what John L. Hulteng had said : In fact, it may well be that if journalism loses touch with ethical values, it will at that same moment cease to be of use to society, and cease to have any real reason for being. But that, for the sake of us all, must never be allowed to happen.

2

NATIONAL MEDIA POLICY
An Overview

Communication, although is an integral and pervasive ingredient of human society, as essential as farming, industry or environment, and fulfills its basic social, economic, political and cultural need; yet issues like communication policy, strategy and planning are fairly new concepts.

Communication policies and planning are comparatively new and emerging areas, which have received steady attention only during the past two decades. A survey by Sayed A. Rahim of several well known journals of communication from 1966 to 1976, found that the term policy, planning or strategy appeared in the titles or sub-titles of only 0.7 per cent of the articles.

The study in the area of communication policies, trends, implementation, etc. has essentially been promoted through the initiative and efforts of UNESCO which had convened the first Intergovernmental Conference on Communication Policies in 1976. The sixteenth session of the General Conference of UNESCO adopted the programme relating to the analysis of communication policies at different levels—public, institutional, professional in selected countries. Under the above programme, a series of monographs devoted to European communication policies, followed by Latin American and Asian countries, was brought out.

The Indian National Commission for Cooperation with UNESCO initiated a study in respect of Communication Policies in India, which was carried out by M.V. Desai and published in 1977. This was, perhaps, the first such initiative of its kind. Subsequently, this topic was the subject of several seminars, two of which were organised by the Indian Institute of Mass Communication; Seminar on Rural Development and Communication Policies held at Hyderabad in February 1979 and a two-day seminar on, Communication in India : Prospects and Policy, in New Delhi in April 1983. Both these seminars made significant contribution in the form of well researched papers on the subject.

The demand for a National Media Policy has been articulated in various fora from time to time.

The National Commission of Self - Employed Women and Women in the Informal Sector in its report brought out in June 1988 observed:

The Indian Government has yet to come up with a well-formulated national communications policy. The Seventh Plan document claims that "The major thrust of the plan relating to mass media will be to raise the level of people's consciousness and enrich their cultural and social life and make them better informed citizens. It will assist in stepping up the pace of development of programmes and sensitize the people towards national and international events of importance. However, the plan does not clearly spell out how this can be achieved. On 24 May 1987, it was announced that a long term national media policy had been finalized by the Information and Broadcasting Ministry. However, to-date no policy announcement has been made. In the absence of a meaningful communications policy, both the public and the private sector media continue to be governed by commercial norms, giving no visibility to poor labouring women, thereby depriving them the opportunity of being brought into the mainstream of national life and having access to information.

The Consultative Committee attached to the Ministry of Information and Broadcasting in its meetings held in July 1993 also had National Media Policy as one of the agenda items for discussion. The Committee was of the view that a National Media Policy be formulated; although there were differing opinions regarding its form and contents. Subsequently, the Ministry circulated a Note on National Media Policy—A Discussion Paper.

India does not have a well formulated National Media Policy; however, there have been a series of actions and statements from which the glimmers of such a policy can be seen; i. e. News Policy for Broadcast Media, objectives of Doordarshan, Cable TV Network Regulation Bill, etc.

In one of the recent articles on the Art of Governance, Systems Failure in Making Policy, K. Subrahmanyam has said :

> But, then, who in this country knows what our Kashmir policy is or, for that matter, our policy on any other issue— defence, foreign affairs, nuclear, space, economic liberalisation, education, public

health—you name it. When asked to outline our national security policy and cite documentation for it, one defence secretary told the estimates committee that the policy was contained in various ministerial statements in the two Houses and replies to Parliamentary questions. If that is the attitude of our bureaucracy and politicians towards policy making, one is bound to find as many policies as there are ministers in charge. This again may be termed a systems failure—failure of the system of cabinet government in India.

In such a system of government, one does not expect any minister either to attempt to ask what the policy on an issue is, nor to formulate one. The ministers will continue to make banal, off the cuff pronouncements without worrying about their policy implications. Since the name of the game is ad hocism; it does not matter what they say. They are not bothered about being consistent because in the absence of a policy there is nothing to be consistent about.

It is, therefore, imperative that to evolve a system, avoid ad hoc decisions and off-the-cuff pronouncements, and also to decide a proper perspective, direction and thrust for future growth and development of media, it is essential that a well thought out, documented and comprehensive National Media Policy be formulated.

The Chairman of the Press Council of India, A. N. Sen has, however, been of the opinion that it may not be wise to seek to lay down any firm National Media Policy, as the effective implementation of the policy may create more problems than it is likely to solve; although there may not be any difficulty in arriving at a general consensus as to certain norms to be observed by the media instead of seeking to lay down any firm National Media Policy. At the same time, however, Sen observed :

> A policy is generally formulated and adopted for achieving a particular object. In the absence of any such object or fixed goal sought to be attained, there can be no question of framing any policy. A policy adopted for achieving no particular purpose will indeed be meaningless. To properly understand and appreciate whether any National Media Policy is at all necessary at this juncture, we have to bear in mind two important considerations : (1) whether the same can be adopted without interfering with the independence of the media; and (2) exactly what is the object which the media are expected to achieve and what is the purpose which the media seek to serve.

There has been a legitimate feeling that in a pluralistic society like India—multi-lingual, with diverse cultures, standards of education, levels of socio-economic development; media—with its rapidly expanding reach and impact, its role in nation building activities, it may not be feasible to evolve a comprehensive National Media Policy. While inaugurating the Seminar on, Communication in India : Prospects and Policy, in New Delhi in April 1983, the Union Minister for Information and Broadcasting said : The question is whether, as suggested in the background paper prepared by the Indian Institute of Mass Communication, there is need for an institutionalised arrangement for formulating and overseeing the implementation of a national communication policy. A comprehensive policy would have to cover not only the modern mass media but also the other major inputs into the stream of communication in the country; the extension agencies of interpersonal communication in the areas of agriculture and health; and the traditional modes of entertainment and ethical instruction besides the modern stage. I have mentioned only the most important among the communication channels other than the modern mass media. With a Press and a film industry which are wholly free within the limits prescribed in article 19 of the Constitution, and with governments in the States with their own perceptions of the priorities in communication and their own information agencies, besides those of the Central Government, it is a moot question whether a national communication policy document is possible and feasible of formulation and implementation.

However, the comprehensive exercise undertaken by the Government of India in evolving Agricultural Policy for the country likewise, underscores the importance and necessity of evolving National Media Policy as well. Elaborating as to why a policy on a subject like agriculture, which encompasses in itself a vast majority of population of the country, is carried on in different agro-climatic zones under varying and differing conditions; Prime Minister P. V. Narasimha Rao said : It looks very odd that we must be looking for a policy on agriculture after having done agriculture four thousands of years. Why do we need a policy?

For the people of India, agriculture is not just a profession; it is their very life...... Over the last 40 years, there has been such a multiplicity of ideas, multiplicity of approaches and philosophy built into agriculture that we do not know what to do. Today, we need a policy because that would really be steering that wheel to take us in the direction in which the government and the country have to go in the matter of agriculture.

He further said : I want this policy to be exposed to public criticism and public comment as much as possible and as widely as possible........ After all agriculture is not really the immediate concern of the Central Government. Therefore, the exposure of this policy to as large a cross section of farmers as possible is necessary. We must also have some flexibility in the policy so that in the light of the experience, we will be able to fine tune it from time to time.

The reports of several Commissions and Working Groups emphatically stressed the imperative necessity and importance of formulating communication policy.

The Report of the International Commission for the Study of Communication Problems stated : The first Conference on Communication Policies was held in San Jose de Costa Rica in July 1976. It unanimously recommended the formulation of new national and international communication policies, urging in particular that national communication councils be set up, scientific research in this field be developed and national and regional news agencies be established.

The San Jose Declaration adopted on that occasion highlights the fact that communication has today come to be accepted as a pre-eminent factor of national renascence, and at the same time serves as a powerful force in relations between nations. It urged that national communication policies should be conceived in the context of national realities, free expression of thought and respect for individual and social rights. A similar conference held in Kuala Lumpur in February 1979 studied, in the context of Asia and Oceania, all aspects of communication policy and stressed that communication, considered both as a means of affirming a nation's collective identity and an instrument of social integration, has a decisive role to play in the democratization of social relations in so far as it permits the multidirectional flow of both horizontal and vertical messages, both from the media to their public and from this public to the media. This effort to define overall, coherent communication policies at the national and regional levels is to be extended in the coming years to the other regions of the world.

The Report of the Working Group on Autonomy for Akashvani and Doordarshan said: If the broadcast media in India have grown haphazardly it is because their role, as that of the media generally, has not been perceived as part of a well defined national communications policy which embraces everything to do with articulation, including education and culture, and physical movement. Such a judgement may, however, be the gift of hind-sight since "systems analysis" and more particularly "communications policy" are themselves fairly new concepts.

According to Mehra Masani who attributed lack of progress in organised broadcasting to the absence of communication policy thirty — five years after the start of organised broadcasting, radio listening is still very restricted in spite of the extension of the radio network. Why? Because the zeal and enthusiasm have been weakened by the absence of a long term communication policy on the basis of which the extension of the network could be properly planned. Such a policy, taking into account the priorities and the available resources, would have provided the guidelines for development appropriate to the country's needs. In the absence of such policy, the expansion has been hesitant, short sighted and out of step with listeners' demands and requirements. Impromptu decisions, often taken in haste, have led to the present stagnation and lack of balance in the network.

The monograph, Communication Policies in India states: Communication policies are sets of principles and norms established to guide the behaviour of communication systems. They are shaped over time in the context of society's general approach to communication and to the media. Emanating from political ideologies, the social and economic conditions of the country and the values on which they are based, they strive to relate these to the real needs for and the prospective opportunities of communication.

Communication policies exist in every society, though they may sometimes be latent and disjointed, rather than clearly articulated and harmonized. They may be very general, in the nature of desirable goals and principles, or they may be more specific and practically binding. They may exist or be formulated at many levels. They may be incorporated in the constitution or legislation of a country; in overall national policies, in the guidelines for individual administrations, in professional codes of ethics as well as in the constitutions and operational rules of particular communication institutions.

Since media policies impinge upon a large number of departments and ministries : Planning Commission, Ministries of Information and Broadcasting, Agriculture, Health and Family Welfare, Education development agencies, media watchdog and regulatory bodies including Press Council, NGOs; print media organisations and institutions, advertising and marketing agencies, film industry, performing and art groups; it would be essential to interest and involve these institutions and organisations at various levels of policy formulation. Without such an elaborate and detailed exercise, media policy formulation would at best be half baked and an incomplete document.

Objectives of National Media Policy

The media structure of each country is dictated by its own special needs and national objectives. Whereas all developing countries have, more or less, similar and common media requirements and objectives, each country may have its special problems and needs. Referring to these, Mankekar pointed out: India is a country of sub-continental size, with a federal structure and gigantic population, with a multiplicity of distinctive cultures, languages, races and religions, with three-fourths of the population living in the villages. It is specially concerned with problems of national integration, political stability, population explosion and liquidation of poverty and illiteracy. These problems must inevitably receive the highest priority in India's programme of nation building, and therefore, the fashioning of a communication media infrastructure for India must have for its objective a concerted attack on these problems. Most of these problems are also common to all the developing countries of Asia, though in varying emphasis and degree.

National Media Policy, according to Pran Chopra, should help media fulfil the objectives of providing access to information to the largest number of people, preserve their credibility and work as two-way channel. He defines National Media Policy as under:

By national policy I am only going to mean those decisions of the national government which might help the media fulfil functions that are appropriate for them in a democratic and pluralistic country like India. I consider four functions of the media to be the most appropriate in the Indian context. First, the media should provide to the largest number of people easy access to information which is reliable, relevant, and abundant. Second, the media must provide reasonably free channels of expression for opinions which are well informed, responsible and adequately reflect all relevant points of view. Third, media should be a two-way channel: not only addressing messages to the audience but also giving the audience a forum for the expression of its concerns. The fourth overrides all these three functions: the media must preserve their credibility.

Given the complex nature of emerging media scenario, expectations of making significant contribution to nation building, and the impact on society that media has, it is indeed extremely difficult to assign specific objectives for any Media Policy. Recognising the immense difficulties that media scholars, policy makers and communication experts are encountered within this context the question remains: why not at least a systematic effort at evolving comprehensive National Media Policy. Pointing out to the failure of the government for not coming up with a comprehensive communication policy, Masani says: Government considered it appropriate to get Parliament's approval to its Industrial policy and its Scientific policy through resolutions on both but it has not thought fit to obtain Parliament's concurrence to its Communication Policy—if there is one. In the absence of such a policy, the media under Government control are treated by the Government itself as agencies to publicise and defend Government decisions and actions. There is no clear perception of the purpose the media are intended to serve, nor of their role in the process of development. This results in hasty and often incorrect decisions being taken in the face of rapid technological developments. The absence of a national policy affects the performance of our representatives at international meetings called by the ITU, UNESCO, the UN and others. Delegates from India drawn from different ministries and organisations pursue different policies at different conferences because such technical questions as management of frequency allocations or copyright in broadcast material cannot be discussed in a vacuum.

It is not easy to devise media policy for a country as large and varied as ours, broken up into so many linguistic regions. Media Policy is not an end in itself but consists of sets of principles which emanate from the political, social and economic conditions of society. Addressing the "One Asia" Assembly in February 1973 the then Minister of Information and Broadcasting declared that a realistic communications policy in a developing society involves striking a balance between three factors—what is socially desirable, what is economically meaningful, and what is technologically feasible. What is the policy which has been framed on these principles? This is still to be made known.

The emerging media scenario in the country, being strengthened by developments in the telecommunication sector, expansion in regional press, rising literacy figures, social and political awareness; role of voluntary media organisations in acting as "facilitators", recognition of significant contribution that the media is capable of making in nation-building, has made it incumbent that requisite action be initiated in formulating comprehensive National Media Policy.

It is hoped that the succeeding chapters in the book would help crystalise some of the issues in the discussion on this subject.

NOTE

In the chapter various terms, communication, communications and information have been used. We would like to refer to the following for clarification :

I. **Report of the International Commission for the Study of Communication Problems (1982)**—In Appendix I–General Comments, one of the members, Sergel Losev points out :

The term "communication" was not properly defined and this tended to mar our Report terminologically. Communication and information, communication and mass media are often mixed up. It is especially regretful that due to this too wide a definition of the term "communication" the problems of information were not adequately dealt with. In many cases still one should read "information" when it is written "communication".

In Appendix II — Notes, the Commission clarifies : Definitions of several general notions dealt with in this Report—more particularly, those of communication and information—have not been standardized nor is there a unanimity as to their meanings. In fact, the terms are used by different authors in a variety of ways, with many nuances regarding their components and significance. Nevertheless, information is often basically considered to be the signs or coded messages transmitted in one direction from a source to a receiver, while communication corresponds more to the complexity of the phenomenon of various interchanges, through signs and symbols, between individuals or communities.

It must be said that in a part of the literature, the two terms information and communication are often confused or used indiscriminately. In the preceding Report, the terms have been used as consistently as possible to refer to two different phenomena : Communication as the process of exchanging news, facts, opinions, messages between individuals and people; Information as the "product" i.e. news, data, and various other contents and outputs of media, cultural activities or industries.

II. The Note on National Media Policy–A Discussion Paper by the Ministry of Information and Broadcasting, has clarified :

At the outset, the question of nomenclature must be settled, for this present policy has been variously termed by both the Government and those demanding it, at various points of time, as a Media Policy, an Information Policy and as a Communication Policy. Needless to say, all these convey possibly different meanings. Information would include, perforce, a settlement of the debate on the right of access of the individual citizen to information within and without Government, and the enactment of laws to facilitate this as is the practice in many developed countries. A Communication Policy would deal largely with subject matter that is mainly the concern of the present day communication network under the Ministry of Communication and other scientific departments. For the present purpose, it would be advisable that the term 'Media Policy' which will naturally include elements relating to both information and communication, be used to define Government's relationship with the Press, the film media, radio and television, and other media units under the Ministry of Indormation and Broadcasting.

The terms 'Communications' or 'Communication Policies', have been used in the context of relevant text.

The communication policies of other countries like USA, UK, etc. should have been launched to support an argument that there is a need for well formulated communication policy.

REFERENCES

Bhagat, H. K. L. (1983). Communication in India : Prospects and policy. *Communicator.* July & Oct., pp.3-5.

Chopra, Pran (1986). National Media Policy—New Blood and Old Data Must Flow. *Media Monitor,* Sept.-Oct. 1 (4) : 10.

International Commission for the Study of Communication Problems (1982). Many Voices One World, UNESCO, pp.40-41.

Mankekar, D. R. (1978). Modern Systems of Communication : Problems and Prospects. *Media Asia,* 5 (3) : 142.

Masani, Mehra (1976). *Broadcasting and the People.* National Book Trust, India, New Delhi. pp.7, 164-65.

Ministry of Information & Broadcasting (1994). Note on National Media Policy—A Discussion Paper.

Ministry of Information &Broadcasting (1978). A Report of the Working Group on Autonomy for Akashwani & Doordarshan. p.15.

P. V. Narasimha Rao (1993). A Comprehensive Policy for Agriculture. Directorate of Advertising and Visual Publicity, Ministry of Information and Broadcasting, p. 2.

National Commission on Self-Employed Women and Women in the Informal Sector (1988)-Report.

Sen, A. N. (1986). National Media Policy—Norms Better than Broad Rigid Terms. *Media Monitor,* May-June, pp.5-6.

Subrahmanyam, K. (1994). Art of Governance—Systems Failure in Making Policy. *Times of India,* 8 November.

Syed, A. Rahim (1977). Introduction : The Scope of Communication Policy and Planning Research. In: Syed A. Rahim and Johan Middleton (eds.), *Perspectives in Communication Policy and Planning,* Honolulu, Hawaii, East-West Center, Communication Monographs, Number 3, p. 5.

UNESCO (1977). Communication Policies in India—A study carried out and written by M. V. Desai.

3

TOWARDS AN EMERGING INFORMATION SOCIETY

Some Policy Issues

One of the most profound changes that the contemporary Indian society has been witnessing during the nineties is— transition from an industrial society to an Information Society. This ongoing transition has an all embracing impact on several segments— economy, living styles, entertainment industry, industrial production.

The rapid pace at which the media landscape is changing is the result of convergence of telecommunication, computing and micro-electronics, which is termed as Information Technology. It is the increasing application of Information Technology, as a determining factor, in social and economic issues, that is heralding the country rapidly towards Information Society. India has already begun to chart its course towards the attainment of Information Society with the convergence of computer-oriented communication technologies and its wide ranging application in telecommunication.

The boom in satellite and cable television, proliferation of TV channels, introduction of cellular and paging services; India World on Internet—the largest international network connecting 30 lakh computers; all these are signs that the Information Society has eventually arrived in the country. In this India is in good company of other advanced countries, for example, Britain, which recently took a giant step towards a digital future in its race to catch up with America.

Britain entered the age of 24 hour TV shopping. The remote retailing portends the death of traditional shopping. A test programme on the home shopping channel even allows viewers to order goods with a remote control handset. Interactive TV is already on the horizon. The menage—a trois of computer, telephone and consumer electronics is being enlarged.

The concept of Information Society—a world marked by an ever increasing flows of electronic information—is complex and still evolving itself due to its varying manifestations. Some of the protagonists of Information Society consider the emerging developments in computer data bases and telecommunication as the beginning of a new world where the society would be progressively knowledge or information centered and where work would be conducted efficiently; the sceptics, on the other hand, consider that the developments would result in accentuating the gap between the haves and have-nots and create disparities between the information rich and the information poor.

This concept of Information Society goes back to the Japanese who are generally given credit for coining the Japanese term *Johoka Shakai* in mid-1960s. The term simply means Information Society, in which the primary activity of a majority of work force is in the areas of information production, processing and distribution. In the Information Society, information constitutes the basic resource and information workers are the main segment of employees. Whereas the social scientists consider Information Society as a process of technical change, subsequently it has been defined in terms of work force structure. In the Information Society, a majority of work force is engaged in the production, processing, transmission and distribution of information goods and services. The bewildering advances and developments in computerised information systems have brought the industrialised nations to the brink of what some have begun to describe as post-industrial era of the Information Society. The centrality of information/knowledge has also been emphasised by Daniel Bell.

In the post-industrial society, processing of information will be more important than production of goods. The value of information will be increasingly recognised as will the need for information specialists to act as guides to the vast information resources that will exist in the electronic form. The magnitude and diversity of the electronic resources will place trained information workers in great demand. The ascendancy of information as commodity is becoming apparent even in developing countries, in that majority of labour force in quite a few of these consists of information workers. *Informatization* is becoming a global trend. Information is considered not only as commodity but also as a cultural and social resource. The contemporary society is at a point where information and wealth are practically one and the same thing; information is commodity rather than a public service.

India's Progress Towards Information Society

In India, the concept of Information Society got off to a slow start—a delayed response to the waves of sweeping changes in the outside world. However, the liberal policies of Prime Minister Rajiv Gandhi during 1984-89 ushered in telecommunication and computer revolution in the country. As a result of government support for the development of electronic and telecommunication infrastructure, the information revolution got off to an encouraging beginning in 1980s.

Since 1991, and more so during the recent past the pace of diffusion of technologies, cable and satellite television has gathered momentum at a speed that newspaper articles have been frequently using terms as 'super-information explosion', 'multi-media revolution' and 'information super-high ways' in relation to developments in information technology in India.

It would, however, be interesting and relevant to refer to a seven nation survey conducted amongst college students from different countries in 1987 including India, Japan and US. The survey sought to find out to what extent respondents knew about information society and emerging new media, what they felt about some of the forecasts of life in an information age, and how they related information technology to the solution of problems in their own society. The survey listed the ten new media : One way and interactive cable television, video cassette recorders, video disc players, video text, teletext, facsimile, personal computers, direct broadcast satellite and cellular radios. The students in India belonged to the Delhi and Jawaharlal Nehru Universities. Although the study was explorative in nature, yet it was concluded that the Indian respondents did not feel that technologies can do much to solve the most serious national problems which in India's case were identified as, poverty, education and regional politics.

Satellites

With the rapid expansion of satellite and telecommunication services in India, a number of organisations in the public and corporate sectors, and companies are planning to use satellite communication networks for corporate communication or maintaining computer networks. The Hindu has already become the first Indian newspaper to use satellite transmission facilities for its Delhi edition.

With Intelsat, leasing a portion of capacity of its proposed satellite-2 E, India has entered the global space market in a big way. The indigenously built INSAT-2 E, which is scheduled for launch in the last quarter of 1997 will be used by Intelsat for providing services to its customers. Intelsat is the international intergovernmental cooperative organisation providing telecommunication services for different regions of the world. The media world is unanimous that alliance with Intelsat will catapult India as one of the key satellite TV forces in the region. After the debacle of APSTE-2, this agreement, the first of its kind that the 135 nation Intelsat has signed with an outside agency, is bound to change the TV entertainment scenario in the country.

India's entry into space and boom in satellite capacity over the Indian skies will mean more satellite TV channels in major regional languages and better entertainment and news programmes. With increasing possibility of private entrepreneurs and industry entering the field, to create user-oriented information systems and products, the potential uses of space for information and communication are wide open.

Doordarshan is one of the few television organisations which uses domestic satellites for telecast of national and regional services. The successful launching of INSAT-2B earlier made it possible for Doordarshan to telecast additional TV programmes through domestic satellite; with five transponders on the satellite widening the network's horizon through five new channels.

With the launching of Asia Sat I in April 1990—the major broadcast satellite agency over the Indian airspace—a cable TV Revolution has set in. Asia Sat I's footprints cover most of Asia and parts of the Pacific. STAR TV launched the satellite television service through Asia Sat by the end of 1990. The number of STAR TV homes all over Asia increased rapidly.

Apart from Doordarshan programmes uplinked to the INSAT-2A satellite and the STAR to ASIA SAT, some other networks including CNN and Asia net uplinked to Arab Sat and Ekran also have contributed to the media hype that the country is currently witnessing.

The trail blazing efforts of STAR TV and intense competition to reach for the Asian skies, the satellite industry's revenues are expected to be in the range of $ 30 billion by the year 2000. According to Deodhar, Chairman of the Doordarshan's Airtime Committee: Space over Asia is becoming prime property. The booming economies of many Asian nations like India, China, Indonesia and Malaysia and their prosperous and demanding middle class have fueled a very high degree of interest in satellite communication services. The boom in satellite capacity over Indian skies will mean more satellite TV Channels in all major languages, more entertainment, more news.

Cable Television

With the sudden and spectacular growth of satellite and cable television networks in the country since 1991, India is fast acquiring the attributes of an Information Society. The special edition of India Today, 1991 caught the spirit of the moment when it heralded the arrival of CNN in January and of Star TV in April, both in 1991 as "Easily the most dramatic revolution took place on the TV screen. 1991 was the year when India ended decades of isolation from the rest of the world." It added, "with five channels on offer and round-the-clock broadcasting, prime time was now any time. The spread of cable TV has already given urban household a choice. Star TV decided to the Asian region made it multiple."

Telecommunication and Computer

In addition, efficient, well developed and modern telecommunication system is *sin qua non* with modernity and economic growth, and is one of the important critical inputs to determine the progress and the pace of socio-economic transformation of the society.

Although in the previous Five Year Plans, telecommunication had made considerable strides both in quantity and quality, its growth in India as compared to the developments in the world telecommunication can at best be termed as modest. Even by the standards of many developing countries, India is far behind in providing telecom services to the people. According to Planning Commission, the telephone density in the country at 0.81 per hundred is less than that in China (1.7), Egypt (5.1), Malaysia (7.37) or even Thailand (6). Large population and the huge size of the country have adversely affected the telephone density in India inspite of the fact that telecom network has recorded considerable growth in the recent past, which has been the outcome of the liberal policies of Prime Minister Rajiv Gandhi. The National Telecommunication Policy, announced in May 1994 has revised the goal to provide a telephone on demand by 1997, besides other value-added services made possible by a combination of digital switching and fibre optic transmission. It is also envisaged to provide a range of value-added services : E-mail services, audio and video conferencing services, videotext and bureaufax centres at the sub-divisional or equivalent towns.

Telecommunication services are no longer considered elite services. The simplistic thinking : A man can live without a telephone, but can he survive without drinking water, earlier came in the way of the development of the telecommunication sector. Now the enormous planning and logistics support that an efficient telecom section can provide to all sectors of economy, and the resultant gain in productivity, is being duly taken into account in determining priorities.

A recent study of 199 villages attached to 32-C-DOT RAXs conducted by the National Council for Applied Economic Research estimates Rs. 70,000 net economic benefit from each rural telecom line. The flow of information from distant markets might permit new cropping patterns which in turn would generate higher incomes; or access to information might lead to reduction of inventories which would translate to higher profits.

A quiet revolution in computers got underway during the late nineties. The revolution, inspired by Rajiv Gandhi; the computers were all over several government offices, companies and in utility services. For almost a decade now, computer had begun revolutionising the life styles in homes, offices, business and elsewhere.

India has established regional and national computer networks that seek to meet a large number of needs. As large systems are considered more cost effective, the government has been promoting such centres. Three important networks established by the government are : NICNET to serve central and state governments; INDONET to serve public and service sectors and commercial organisations and EDUNET to serve educational and training institutions.

NICNET is the most visible, the most extensive network of the government. The nationwide information network, NICNET, is a satellite based information service developed for its operations at the central, state and district levels. The network helps decision making for social, economic and development planning and implementation and project monitoring. It represents an advanced level institutional application of information technology to planning and provides a model of a centrally planned approach to information services. Several other networks have also been pressed into service thus widening the base for accessing remote information and communication through electronic mail, computer conferencing, teletext, facsimile, etc. The two important research and cooperative computer networks which India is making use are : CARINET, a network among development related organizations around the world (including Australia, Canada, Japan, Philippines, Singapore) providing information related to agriculture, health education, human rights, disaster relief etc.; and ERNET, an experimental network linking education and research institutions in India.

Given the size of information explosion, computer in India has established its primacy as an indispensable tools for monitoring and planning development plans. The computer revolution, sweeping the country, has made its impact felt even in the hinterland districts where mass of data generated are gathered and organised for decision making at state level.

During the past decade, most of the telecom computer and micro-electronic technologies which constitute the bed rock of Information Society, have expanded rapidly in the country. The high technology development has been aided by India's vast pool of technically trained and scientific man power, wave of liberalisation in economic policies, virtually sweeping the country and trend towards market economy. This expansion, however, is confined to largely metropolitan cities, and in some cases state headquarters and large towns.

Social Implications of Information Society — Some Policy Issues

A very large percentage of the population, living in small towns and villages, is not touched by these developments, raising several socio-cultural and economic issues, which have to be reckoned with. The extent to which beneficient aspects, which some of these technologies claim for society, could find application in nation building, need closer examination. It would, therefore, be important to go beyond the hype and euphoria, as also the state of optimism generated by the expanding entertainment industry and information technology, which are essentially led by market forces. What are the implications of the emerging Information Society for the common man and a lay citizen in the country, what do we do about the yawning gap, increasing by the day, between the information rich and the information poor and what do these information societal changes sportend for the future.

During the world's biggest telecommunications exhibition organised by the ITU in Geneva in October 1983, the chairman of the world's largest operator of telecommunication, Charles L Brown, made some very pertinent and interesting remarks on the subject matter of the seminar, ... a revolution is taking place in communications technology. Innovation in telecommunications technology is proceeding at a dizzying pace, creating a dazzling array of new products, services and capabilities. Each new generation of technology tends to offer not only greater speed, capacity and versatility in the transporting and processing of information but also lower unit costs. The driving force of this revolution, of course, is the convergence of communications and computer technology which is literally redefining the telecommunications industry...... Fundamental changes are starting to occur in our concepts of telecommunications. No longer is a telephone simply an instrument for voice communications but rather an information terminal, a means of assessing and exchanging information in a variety of ways, to and from a variety of sources. No longer is television simply a passive instrument for receiving news and entertainment but rather an interactive communications device, visually displaying transactions that are taking place electronically. However, mentioning some of the complex issues that we face while we march through the development process, Brown said :

> How can we see to it that the information revolution does not bypass the lesser developed countries of the world, as was the case with the industrial revolution?
>
> How can we effect the transfer of communication technology from the haves to the have-nots under terms that are affordable to those who need it and equitable to those who invested so heavily to create it?
>
> How can we accommodate increased diversity in services and supplies without excessive fragmentation of national and international communications infrastructures?

The eminent sociologist, Kothari (1993) in Growing Amnesia has highlighted the fact that the state is playing an increasingly diminishing interventionist role and it has been left to be decided by market forces as to what is good for the people. Pointing to the burgeoning consumerist society which is only concerned with the gratification of individuals. Kothari says : Social equity has been for all practical purposes, sacrificed at the altar of development models that are designed to modernise society in terms of technology and science.

In this context Kishore (1944) points out : The middle class elite in India whose life styles resemble that of the super rich anywhere in the world are at a comparative advantage over access to information and entertainment. The internal contradictions in present day India are stark clear : industrialised cities and marginally subsistent villages; jet planes and bullock carts; satellite technology and lack of clean drinking water, cellular telephones and absence of even one telephone in every village. This dualism has widened the gap between the rich and the poor.

According to Karnik and Chitnis (1984), our communication practice reflects the powerful pressure of the *nouveau-riche*; and communication has played an important role in promoting a value system corresponding to the style of life of the most aggressive sections of this new class. Sexist and sadistic violence, glorification of the ruthless go-getter, lure of the latest material gadgets are almost idealised by the emerging software linked with commercial agencies.

An important study by Srivastava (1987) which has been frequently cited, to underline the socio-economic and political implications and issues, and future trends of television ownership and viewership in India in the year 2000, indicates that the rapid television expansion in the country will accentuate the knowledge gap between the poor in urban areas and the rich on the one hand, and between rural and urban people on the other. The study points out:

1. As urban viewers would constitute the majority of the viewers, they would demand the kinds of programmes which are entertainment based, rather than those which play the role of a development communication tool.
2. There will be perpetual conflict between programmes meant for rural and urban poor and those suitable for middle and upper income brackets in urban areas.
3. In terms of political implications, the vast majority of rural masses would not have access to TV. Thus, the TV's role for integration and unity of the country and as an equaliser of regional differences would not be achieved.
4. The people who would have access to TV would already have high media exposure from newspapers, radio, video and movies. The media poor would not be able to afford most of the means of receiving external information through electronic media. Thus, the knowledge gap between haves and have-nots would widen.

The study also suggests several measures to meet the situation including governmental intervention in the existing market structure so as to reduce the price of second hand black and white television sets for the poorer sections of the population, provision of community TV sets in rural areas and urban slums and introduction of TV sets in schools at public cost.

Information technology and telecommunication has raised renewed hopes for enhancing national development. Telecom wizards and professionals like Sam Pitroda are die hard optimists in 'promising potential and beneficial outputs of the technologies of tomorrow'. *Infotainment* and *Infotech* are the buzz words of the day which are increasingly overtaking terms like *Devcom*.

Even in the field of education, where with the introduction of new communication technologies, a teacher has to adapt to the role of a manager, facilitator and organiser of knowledge, there is an under-current of scepticism among some educators that adoption of technology may lead to further elitism of education widening the gap between haves and have-nots. Adoption of technology needs a lot of resources which every institution cannot afford. The government cannot provide every student with necessary facilities. This, it is feared, will create a new elite class rapidly, if technology is used selectively.

In their seminal book, *The Information Society—A Retrospective View* (1993), Herbert S. Dordick and Georgette Wang have made an attempt 'to revisit the claims that have been made for the emerging Information Society'. One of the paragraphs reproduced below heralds then dawn of a new millennium a brave young world, full of promise and prosperity.

> The explosive diffusion of computers, telecommunications, broadcast and video media, and the information media is seen in national and global statistics. Almost half of the workers in the industrialized world are employed by the rapidly growing information industries, and in almost every industry there are workers, whose primary tasks are to create, collect, process, and distribute information. The value added of information products and services to the United State GNP is, today, slightly greater than 45 per cent and for Europe and Japan somewhat more than 40 per cent. The world information industry, even if narrowly defined, will be greater than $ 500 billion before the end of the decade. The production, processing, and distribution of information is a major industry throughout the world. By the year 2000, it will account for about 40 per cent of the world's industrial production.

However, doubts and scepticism sets in almost immediately as to the efficacy of the newly emerging dispensation to the Third World nations. The nagging issues of widening gulf between the information rich and the information poor as also between the haves and have-nots start emerging as under:

> If there is a growing gap between the production and consumption of information there is, perhaps, an even greater gap between what have come to be known as the information rich and the information poor. Information technology and modern telecommunications

raised renewed hopes for enhancing national development. Development information replaced development communications as the mechanism for stimulating growth in the developing and newly industrializing countries. Whether development information can be a catalyst for development is a moot point in many countries, where reliable telephone or even telegraph communications are rarely available, and where computers are only in the dreams of young people returning from studying in advanced countries. Plagued by barriers of poverty, poor health, low life expectancy, illiteracy, and little access to tertiary education, emerging countries must compete with advanced countries in a highly competitive global marketplace. What does the information society mean to them? Economic growth in the least-developed nations of the world has stagnated or has been increasing very, very slowly. The gap between the developed and lesser developed nations continues to widen annually. Can these Third World nations ever catch up?

It is, therefore, most essential to stress that while laying down national media policy, the government and bureaucrats of the Information and Broadcasting Ministry are not swayed by a mind set conditioned by the newly emerging, dazzling spectrum of technologies like paging service, 61-television channels, information superhighways, etc.

It has always been adequately stressed, acknowledged and accepted that technology is not a panacea for all the ills of the society. However, since information technology, information economy and information society (increasingly dominated by media entertainment industry) have visible manifestation and are an important part of our daily lives, we tend to forget the wider social implications for that section of society which is being increasingly marginalised, in the wake of onward march towards global economy and market forces. No national media policy could afford to ignore this section of society which lives on the periphery of modern day existence.

REFERENCES

Brown, Charles L. (1987). Revolution in Communication Technology, *Media Asia* 13 (1).

Chatterjee, Saibal (1993). Fast Forward—Special Report. *Times of India*, October 31.

Goonasekera, Anura (1993). Media Technology and Social Imperatives : An Examination of Communication Polices in Selected Asian Countries. *Media Asia* **20** (4): 194-204.

Hudson, Heather, E. (1993). Maximizing Benefits from New Telecommunication

Technologies : A Development Based Approach to Communications Planning. *Media Asia,* **20** (3): 133-149.

Jamias, Juan F. (1993). The Impact of New Communication Technologies on Cultural Identity in Rural Asia. *Media Asia,* **20** (4) : 205-207.

Jussawalla, Meheroo (1993). Information Technology and Economic Development in the Asia-Pacific. *Media Asia,* **20** (3) : 127-132.

Khan, Rahat Nabi (1987). The Third Industrial Revolution : An Economic Overview. *Impact of Science on Society,* **146** : 115-122, UNESCO.

Kishore, Krishana (1994). The Advent of STAR TV in India: Emerging Policy Issues. *Media Asia* **20** (2): 96-103.

Lee, Chang Seek and Ely D. Gomez. (1992). The Contribution of the Information Sector to the Industrial Growth of Korea. *Media Asia,* **19** (3): 156-168.

Mowlana, Hamid and Laurie, Wilson J. (1988). Communication Technology and Development. Reports and Papers on Mass Communication No. 101: UNESCO.

Rao, P. V. (1994). High Way to Nowhere. *Indian Express,* July 21.

Singhal, Arvind and Rogers, Everett, M. (1989). *India's Information Revolution,* New Delhi : Sage.

Smith, Roger, B. (1987). The Twenty-First Century Corporation. *Impact of Science on Society,* **146**: 177-182, UNESCO.

Thomas, P. N. (1993). Informatization and Change in India—Cultural Politics in a Post-Modern Era. *Asian Journal of Communication,* **3** (1): 64-83.

Thomas, Sunny. (1994). Information Highways to Success. *Times of India,* June 22.

Wang, Georgette. (1991). Information Society in Their Mind : A Survey of College Students in Seven Nations. *Asian Journal of Communication,* **1** (2): 1-18.

Wang, Georgette. (1993). Satellite Television and the Future of Broadcast Television in the Asia-Pacific. *Media Asia,* **20** (1): 140-151.

4

MEDIA POLICY AND NATION BUILDING

The question of evolving the national media policy has been engaging the attention of media scholars, government functionaries and public persons for quite some time now. However, the aspect of nation building which should be the foremost objective of the media policy does not figure either in the Discussion Paper or in the Questionnaire issued by the Ministry of Information and Broadcasting.

The problem of nation building is related to the transformation of parochial (local, communal or religious) loyalties into national loyalties i.e. identification with the State. It means the achievement of national integration for which we, in India, have been endeavouring since the attainment of independence but have not yet fully succeeded. Theoretically speaking, the task of nation building involves two major issues : first, it involves the creation of a public authority which can legitimately assert itself throughout the national territory, secondly it involves the creation of an integrated national community. However, both the issues are integrally linked, they are the two sides of the same coin. A public authority can only be legitimate if throughout the territory of the state, if a certain level of integrated national community exists and participates in the social, political, economic, cultural processes generated by the public authority through the creation of relevant structures throughout the length and breadth of the state. There are, however, numerous factors that determine nation building. The process of nation building in any specific country must also take into account the peculiarities, specificities, the goals set by the policy makers and planners, the objective limitations imposed by the historical development of the social, economic, cultural and political structures and processes. We shall discuss these and the media policy, as playing an effective and facilitative role, in helping the process of nation building and development in general, with special emphasis in the context of India.

Before we discuss all this and the complex relationships it creates, it is pertinent to discuss what do we mean by Development. The term has been interpreted in various ways by sociologists, economists and development planners. Todaro (1977) has described it as a complex of social, cultural attitudes and economic changes for which we should strive for the fulfilment of basic needs of the people. He says, "Development must be conceived as a multi-dimensional process evolving major changes in social structures, popular attitudes and national institutions as well as the acceleration of economic growth, the reduction of inequality and eradication of poverty. Development must be turned to the diverse basic needs and desires of individuals and social groups". According to Goulet (1971) there are three components of development : Life sustenance, self-esteem and freedom. All the three components are equally important, but the first, life sustenance, is fundamental. Without the means of fulfilling primary needs such as food, clothing, shelter, health, education and employment, no human being can have self-esteem. To a person who is poor and has no self-esteem, freedom will have no meaning. Rogers (1976) has defined development as a "Participatory process of social change in society intended to bring about both social and national advancement for the majority of the people through them gaining greater control over their environment."

Development has been defined differently by different people but we can say that it broadly entails and suggests a process of change that is multi-dimensional—social, economic, cultural, political, etc. It also entails a change in their structures and attitudes. The change ought to create a more culturally homogenous and consesual society endeavouring to enhance progress and capability so that the basic economic needs like food, shelter, clothing, education and health can be fulfilled. Development also entails the creation of structures and processes for the participation of groups and individuals in whole process of contemplated change so that they become an integral part of the whole process and their consent is assumed to have been taken into account. Therefore, development can be said to be an all embracing concept encompassing economic, social, cultural, educational and political aspects of the society. It is the sum total of alround balanced and planned growth.

Generally speaking, national development must, therefore, focus on mobilizing human potential through (a) access to material resources like good health, education, housing and food; and (b) creation of a culture and environment that guarantees freedom, human rights and personal self-respect. The World Bank Economist, Dr. Mahabub-ul-Haq has developed a report on Human Resource Development for different countries of the world. He developed certain measures and indicators to determine the standard of living and growth of human resources. These indicators include expenditure on health, sanitation, education, research and nutrition.

Thus, we see that the process of nation building and development is integrally linked and overlap in so many ways. Nation building entails essentially the creation of public authority within the national territory by the creation of relevant social, economic, cultural and political structures and also a homogeneous community which would essentially be a cultural or additional phenomenon of commitment to the state. Similarly, development implies the structural and cultural aspects of change and transformation but it also implies a certain concretization of factors and indicators for different countries. It, therefore, means to identify a stage at which the changes in different aspects of society, economy and polity complement each other so that the process of nation building can continue smoothly. Nation building and development, being complementary concepts, reinforce each other.

In case of India the nation building process has been identified around the creation of a realm of central values as embodied in the preamble of the constitution in the creation of a secular, socialist and democratic society. For the realisation of these central values relevant sometimes at social, economic and political levels have been created to permeate the society and integrate through linkage the peripheral groups and individuals who either do not know of the central values or are opposed to it. This would thus create a difficult situation for the creation of an integrated political community. Thus, the process of nation building in general, and particularly in India, would entail removal of caste, religions, ethnic, regional inequalities, decentralized planning by involving local groups and leaders de-tribalization of a large section of the population, removal of inequalities and disparities in income, wealth, employment among groups, creation of political and administrative machinery free from vested interests, land reforms curbing the growth of monopolies and concentration of means of production in fewer hands, gender in - equality, etc.

Development Communication

The role of development communication or mass media becomes important here to create the relevant kind of consciousness and awareness among the people keeping in view the goals, the limitations and priorities of the nation. It also becomes important in so far as it can play a positive and creative role in educating the masses as well as policy makers and planners about the weaknesses and bottlenecks emerging in the process of change. The media in such a situation can mediate to resolve the knot through creative suggestions and in–depth analysis and understanding of such a situation for which an elaborate and well thought out communication development policy is required.

The development communication can be defined as a deliberate, systematic and continuous effort to organise human activity for the efficient use of communication resources and for the realisation of communication policy, in the context of a particular society's developmental goals, means and priorities and subject to its prevailing forms of economic, social and political organisation. A commonly used definition given by Nora C. Quebral :

> Development communication is the art and science of human communication applied to a speedy transformation of a country from poverty to a dynamic state of economic growth and social equality and the larger fulfilment of the human potential.

Rajni Kothari (1988) has laid out:The development communication has to be thought of not as a specialized concern but as part and parcel of the struggle for human liberation, freedom and justice, strengthening the struggles of communications and cultures, of national entities that are thoughtful to be marginalized, and of already marginalized people within these and other societies. It should be communication that exposes the hypocrisy of the rhetoric in international forums, which is in direct contrast to the same state's behaviour in their own societies. Communication should be a process that contains the forces of backlash and promotes the forces of transformation and survival.

Development communication implies desirable changes in the thinking and working of the people. To be more specific, it grows mostly out of people's participation and people's satisfaction. It is purposive communication for planned change and intended to promote human development which basically means that communication will help reduce poverty, unemployment and social inequality. It is communication with a social conscience.

The general paradigm of development communication today indicates the broad outlines of an outlook followed by developed, developing and the under - developed countries but since the paradigm lays stress on identification of goals, means, priorities subject to the country's social, economic and political organisation, it must be correctly and precisely identified in the case of India. Having identified the socio-economic and political structures, the inequalities, the goals and means, etc. can be assigned a definite transformatory role or direction.

I think what development communication would include in the Indian context cannot proceed unless we have identified the direction of social, economic and political transformation since its role is facilitative.

The dominant paradigm of development communication has largely remained a one-way model which is incompatible with a focus on participation of the people . The fall of this dominant paradigm gave way to a 'new' paradigm for development. This new paradigm is pluralistic and its key elements include :

1. Greater equality in the distribution of development investment, information and the consequent socio-economic benefits of focussing on such weaker sections of the population as the poor women and racial and ethnic minorities.
2. Popular participation, knowledge sharing and empowerment to facilitate self-development efforts by individuals, groups and communities.
3. Self-reliance and independence in development, emphasizing the potential of local resources, self-reliance became a key concept at both the national and local levels, implying that every nation and perhaps every village, could develop in its own way.
4. Integration of traditional and modern communication systems and the use of 'little media' alongwith the 'big media' of television and films in order to facilitate development.

The new paradigm of development was framework in which communication played a facilitative role. Self-development approaches to development communication led to more popular participation, man mobilization and group efficacy with greater responsibility for development planning and execution at the local level. The main roles of mass communication in such self-development are : to provide technical information about development problems and possibilities, and about appropriate innovations, and to inculcate wide information about self development accomplishments by local groups so that other such groups could project from others' experiences.

Though development communicators have reshaped their thinking but the need for basic indicators regarding food, shelter, clothing, employment, land reforms and health cannot be ignored. Only after considering the primary necessities of life we can further think of development of the nation. There are various factors which can be said to det ermine or influence the process of nation building. We will not take up all the factors but will consider a few which are of utmost importance these days.

Environmental Protection

It is now twenty-three years since the 'environment' was put on the agenda of international concern, with the Stockholm Environment Conference in 1972. Most people understand environment to be limited to only one aspect : pollution. Pollution is only one facet of many sided environmental problem. Environment is not an abstract concern, nor is it just a matter of aesthetics or personal taste. Our physical nature, our mental health, our culture and institutions, our opportunities for fulfilment, our very survival, all of these are directly related to and affected by the environment in which we live. It encompasses a vast range of subjects from resource depletion to the effects of over growing. The aesthetic degradation due to demolition of old buildings and their replacement by multistoreyed blocks, to people inadvertently taking action which will deteriorate their environment, like building huge dams, paving away large stretches of land, boom in tourism, all have bearing on environment related issues like the destruction of trees and movements to build roads, tourism as a source of cultural pollution apart from physical pollution, can provide matter for concern about the environment.

The media played a notable part in carrying forward the message inherent in the *Chipko* movement, which basically is the movement for protecting environment. Today, *Chipko* has become an important word in the lexicon of environmentalists the world over. The *Chipko* movement, which has received sustained media attention in the country, is probably the world's most well known grass roots eco-development movement. *Chipko* activities have attracted the attention of environmentalists, Gandhians, various people interested in the process of social change and the media personnel throughout the world.

The non-violent, action oriented *Chipko* movement has greatly helped unite the people and focus attention on the mismanagement of forest resources. Its Gandhian character has brought to it considerable sympathy. One line of thought is that the main objective of forest management should be soil and water conservation : forests do not bear timber, resin and foreign exchange but soil, water and pure air. The self-sufficiency of the hill people in food, clothing and shelter is important but is secondary to the major ecological objectives. This cannot be achieved unless all commercial green felling is stopped and no new contracts entered into with industrialists to supply raw material. Another philosophy behind the *Chipko* movement is the belief that no conservation is possible without the cooperation of the people. Eco-development strategies will inspire the poor when they are based not just on ecology but also on the needs of the people.

Chipko's message is that man is the child of mother earth. He has every right to suckle at the breasts of mother earth, but not at the cost of mother's health. Soil and water are the flesh and blood of the earth. When we fell trees, we skin the earth, she bleeds. This is a common sight during rains.

Researchers in the Philippine based IRRI warned that environmental degradation and adverse climate conditions are eroding the genetic diversity of rice, which could lead to food shortages for Asia's booming population. The report said that 'Nature's legacy to mankind of diverse genetic resources is risk.' The biological heritage is threatened by the recent rapid pace of change, the undesirable side effects of industrialization and the continuing population expansion.

The number of NGOs, voluntary groups, academic and corporate bodies and social activists, taking interest in environmental awareness has increased significantly in recent years. As Rahul Gupta points out: The environment will not longer be the concern of merely professionals, ecologists and rebels who are eternally questing for a cause. A new breed of seekers has joined the ranks of the ecologically conscious college students. The subject is at last being incorporated in the regular curricular, as a part of the project designed to enhance the environmental expertise of decision makers, policy formulators and tertiary level educators. It will also increase the environmental skills and awareness of tertiary level students and contribute to strengthening the environmental expertise at technical and managerial levels in the region. NGO's also called for evolving and effective strategy to ensure the development of urban habitats in the fragile Himalayas without causing environmental degradation and urged the government to study the impact of dams on ecology before giving clearance. This was concluded in a workshop of non-government organisations on "environment and sustainable development' held at Shimla recently. It also underlined the need for ensuing greater participation of women in environment protection and called for closer co-operation among various voluntary agencies. It stressed the need for reducing the generation of solid waste by promoting the concept of recycling and renewal among the urban inhabitant, besides promoting and preserving the traditional values and cultural heritage. It also suggested that pollution control boards in various states should organise training programmes for voluntary agencies so that these could effectively contribute to check pollution.

The Asahi Glass Foundation has also released the results of its third annual: Questionnaire on Environmental Problems and the Survival of Humankind. It found that since the Earth Summit in June 1992, progress has been made in their own countries in specific areas such as environmental education, government regulations to control the environment and protection of the ozone layer. At the same time, respondents expressed satisfaction with progress in activities undertaken by NGOs—local governments, and citizens' groups in their own countries. However, progress remains inadequate in such crucial areas as desertification, global warming, acid rain, overpopulation and poverty.

Environmental issues are progressively taking a holistic perspective including the increasingly consumeristic life styles, development paradigms, as symbolised by big dams are being challenged. Bahuguna has highlighted this aspect as under:

Protection of environment should not be seen in isolation. Similarly, conservation is not possible till we adopt a life style, which had been developed for generations and reflects the wisdom of the people. Wisdom is the collection of experience, which common people have gained for generations.

Hence what is required is how best to accomplish nation building and development without destroying the environment. The choice of industrial development should be determined keeping in view the environmental needs or limitations i.e. development and adoption of environment friendly technologies. It can also include the corrective methods where such possibilities do not exist. It is, therefore, essential that media policy be evolved in a way that the task of creating consciousness about environmental protection becomes one of the foremost objectives of such policy.

Empowerment of Women

For more than a decade, the term "empowerment" has been widely used in relation to women. The most conspicuous feature of the term is that it contains within it the word power. So, obviously, empowerment is about power, and about changing the balance of power. In every society, there are powerful and powerless groups. Power is exercised in social, economic and political relations between individuals and groups. Thus, the method of gaining control over self, over ideology and the resources which determine power—may be termed as "empowerment." Empowerment, therefore, is a process aimed at changing the nature and direction of systematic forces which marginalise women and other disadvantaged sections is a given context.

Gender justice remains a far cry all over the world as has been highlighted by the Human Development Report 1995 brought out by the UNDP. Though the world as a whole has moved closer to gender equality over the past two decades, there is still no society where women fare as well as men. The annual UNDP report ranks 174 nations using a range of economic and social indicators. The comparisons are based on longevity as measured by life expectancy at birth; educational attainment, as measured by a combination of adult literacy and combined primary, secondary and tertiary educational ratios, and basic purchasing power or standard of living, as measured by real Gross Domestic Product per capita in purchasing power parity terms. The 1995 report compares 130 nations for which comparative data were available for disparities between men and women by creating two new indices. The Gender Related Imbalances in basic health, education and income while the Gender Empowerment Measure reflects women's participation at the political and economic levels.

From the first UN sponsored conference held in Mexico city in 1975, declared as the International Women Year, to Copenhagen in 1980 where the mid decade conference was held, on to Nairobi for the culmination of the Women's Decade Conference in 1985 and now to Beijing for a UN Conference of Women held in September 1995. The period 1975-95 is a high water mark in the history of women's struggle the world over for equal rights in all spheres. Thus, if one looks at the women's scenario in the whole world, one finds that the concept of gender seems to be deeply woven in the concept of knowledge of the world, where women are left behind as non-males and non-human beings.

The condition of Indian women is rather critical. It is said that men's work ends with the setting sun but women's work never. According to a recent study reported by the *Economic Times,* India's rural women work for an average nine hours a day against seven hours by men. In the nine hours, the women cover household work, besides collecting water, fuel and fodder. That's not all. A clear sexual division of labour gives them no relief from household chores even if they go out to work. A hectic schedule like this leaves them little time for themselves. Paucity of time is a major hindrance in the development of rural women. When women have no power, they tend to have more children—as a measure of risk insurance—thus contributing towards population explosion.

More and more women speak out against violence in rural and urban India. The media covers it somewhat sensationally, not in sufficient detail, not consistently nor seriously enough. Rape, incest, dowry, murder, sexual harassment on the streets and in the workplace, during war and armed conflict, in police custody—are all crimes against women and violate their human rights, guaranteed in the UN Charter of Human Rights and in the constitutions of most of the nations. Crimes against women in India are of various forms. India has the largest number of child prostitutes in the world (400,000). The low status of the girl child and lack of economic opportunities in families and communities encourage the kidnapping, selling and prostitution of these young women. Since early 1980, violence in the state of Punjab has left thousands of women traumatised. They were forced to marry terrorists at gun point. Anita Anand reports in the *Times of India* that there are about 9000 widows as a result of this violence.

The 1994 Home Ministry's National Crime Records Bureau show that every 51 minutes a women is sexually harassed. Every 54 minutes she is raped and every 102 minutes there is a dowry death. These are conservative estimates as they do not include crimes that are not reported. In India most people's basic needs are unmet. And even when these are societal, behaviour suggests that women are dispensable. They are treated as mothers, a vital human resource, but not as 'women'. The declining sex ratio is another alarming concern. Demographers believe that the reasons are higher: under enumeration of female in the census, higher mortality rate of women, marked preferences for the male child, leading to the consequent neglect of female infants; the lower status of women at all ages and stages, the adverse impact of frequent child bearing and higher incidence of disease in women. The 1991 census in India reveals how the sex ratio has further declined from 972 in 1901 to 929 in 1991. Nearly 20 crore adult women are illiterate and the ratio of the effective literacy is also insignificant.

Sadly, as reported by Kalhana Feature Service in the *Hindustan Times*, the country paper (a paper prepared by member states for the Beijing Conference so that it could reflect the real situation of women in national reports) merely enumerates the government's schemes and plans without any evaluation of their implementation or their impact on the target group women. The paper is full of empty rhetoric. There were certainly important issues connected with the lives of women which have not been mentioned in the country paper, criminalisation of politics and its impact on women, activities of communal and fundamentalist elements who are creating hurdles in the way of women's progress, and growing violence against women, increasing corruption which is destroying our moral and cultural values and undermining democratic rights.

Uma Ramachandran reports in *The Tribune,* "that it is surprising that in a country so avowedly eager to progress, the question of the status of women is regarded so cooly by the majority of its populace, such matter is looked at askance and fewer people bother to talk about it. In the process, a happily slumbering society is left free to sleep with no strain on its conscience. And that's the price we pay for progress, for in a society where male is male, and female is subservient, the twain of necessity will not meet."

To enable women to fight against their inferior status, it is necessary to empower them by ensuring their participation in decision making bodies at all levels. Media policy should encourage women to participate in politics. The media should evolve strategies so that the women could be brought into the mainstream of national development not as beneficiaries but as contributors and partakers alongwith men. There is an imperative need to handle the problem of women in all its dimensions.

The strategies that can be suggested to meet the challenges are— developing policies and programmes for the poor, keeping in view the needs of women. Measures should be taken for redistribution of productive assets to improve the resource base of poor, women saved from exploitation, income generating opportunities and productive employment for women; developing institutional framework which promotes high degree of decentralisation and active participation in the community, especially women. Social processes that help women to organise themselves better, should be encouraged so that they can identify their needs. Law and media remain important components for liberalising women from their bindings. So, any attempt at raising the status of rural women should focus on reorganising their work schedule to make optimum use of time. More time at their disposal would give women access to resources like education and gainful employment. This would enhance their status.

Improving women's access to appropriate technology can significantly reduce their workload and can improve efficiency in both basic household and agricultural chores leading to enhanced productivity. A reduction in the workload will also reduce their dependence on more helping hands in the form of more children, thus bringing down fertility levels. Some of the initiatives taken by the government to make women economically independent and self reliant, like *Mahila Samridhi Yojana* and *Rashtriya Mahila Kosh* need to be given due coverage in the media.

For the building of the nation it is important that the women of India should be assertive and visible decision makers before we usher into the 21st century. Hari Jai Singh*, Editor of the *Tribune*, felt that the media could play a very significant role to make society realise the long lasting repercussions of gender bias in a wider perspective.

Consumer Protection

Consumer protection assumes great significance in today's complex market economy, especially so in Third World Countries. The New Economic Policy has opened floodgates to multi-nationals to produce for the Indian market in the name of improving the quality of products in India. As a result, the competing products are using the most modern techniques of advertisement to push up their sales. The consumer has been opened upto the markets in such a way that he finds it sometimes difficult to make the right choice. The variety and number of goods in the market creates an urge in him to acquire as many goods as possible. The consumer runs for the products one after the other. This general psychology of the masses to acquire more goods becomes the main aim and ambition of life, which we call as consumerism. This rat race, a consequence of modern advertisements and the liberal economic policy, also allows space for spurious products to be sold on the market. This is more prominent in developing countries and particularly in our country where small entrepreneurs or those wanting to make fast buck sometimes keep up their sales to earn more profit by adopting unfair means. This development has given rise to the consumer protection movement to protect innocent consumers against being cheated in the market on account of exhorbitant prices, adulteration, underweight and sale of poor quality goods. Just as the producer has the right to design the product, distribute, advertise and price it, the consumer has the right not to buy it. Though the veto power rests with the consumer, it is difficult for him to exercise this in the best interest, due to lack of information or misinformation.

The developing countries are going for industrialization which is an important indicator of development and modernization but the proportion it has assumed in the modern day context, particularly in India, with liberalisation policy, is that it makes the most important criterion of development or modernization. Creating goods in abundance without providing legal checks can lead to disillusionment among people. The ensuring discontent can also pose problem for nation building.

*Keynote Address in the Seminar on 'Gender Concerns in Mainstream Media : Beijing and Beyond', held at Chandigarh on 24 June 1995.

The consumer movement first started in the United States in 1900 and later spread gradually to other parts of the world. It came to India in 1966. The major issues to be tackled are : excessive pricing, short weights and measures, poor performance of the product, lack of safety, high cost of packing, misleading advertising, non-punctuality of supply, poor warranty service and environment pollution. The first consumer movement in India was started by Mrinal Gore, a social worker in Bombay, who demonstrated against the scarcity of water, food stuff and increased prices. The Consumer Association and Consumer Protection Cells emerged thereafter in metropolitan and other cities. It is a movement to protect the consumer against various types of malpractices, exploitation and atrocities indulged in by a number of businessmen and industrialists on the consumers and the consequent need to provide safeguard to these consumers from the clutches of the exploiters in the business and the industrial world.

Consumer movement is aimed at regulating the products or services, methods and standards of manufacturers, sellers and advertisers in the interest of buyers. Such regulation may be institutional, statutory or embodied in a voluntary code accepted by a particular industry or it may result more indirectly from the influence of consumer organisation (*Encyclopaedia Brittanica*, 1990) .

The year 1986 was a landmark year for the consumer movement in India with the passing of the CPA by the Parliament. The 1986 Act was further amended subsequently to further strengthen the consumer movement in the country and is drafted in simple language. It is not tied up in legalese, with umpteen clauses and sub-clauses. It is an important piece of legislation in safeguarding the interest of consumers. The Act is applicable to all goods and services unless otherwise stated by the government. It is applicable to enterprises falling in the categories of public sector financial institutions and cooperative societies. The provisions are in addition to and not in derogation of provisions of other laws. The Act is a comprehensive legislation with its main thrust on giving speedy redressal and compensation to the consumers. Some of the benefits available under this Act are: speedy and cheap relief to the consumers by the authorities, avoids procedural delay, consumer need not consult legal expert, relief is provided on the fundamental principle of natural justice an d it also extends adequate compensation to the aggrieved party. The Act provides for setting up of a quasi-judicial machinery with a three-tier set up- District Forum, State Commission and the National Commission.

The consumer courts function in an informal way. There is no fee involved in filing a complaint and even a letter will serve the purpose.

The only condition is that the name and address of the complainant and the party against whom the complaint is lodged should be given alongwith the gist of grievances and the relief sought. It can be filed in any regional language or English. The complainant can be present for the hearing and there is no need for him to engage a lawyer.

In India, there are nearly 320 consumer organisations. These are mostly concentrated in urban areas. These organizations have been taking a keen interest in consumer problems. The role of the government in consumer education is both direct and indirect. It directly imparts knowledge through government media—Akashvani and Doordarshan give not only theoretical concepts but also show the problems confronting the consumers. The government observes 'quality month' every year in November and March 15 is 'consumer day'. On such occasions newspapers publish reports and articles. Seminars, conferences and lectures are also organized.

The setting up of the National Consumer Council is another step towards helping the consumer. Many state governments have taken appropriate measures by setting up consumer affairs cells. Arya (1994) observed that to take the consumer movement to the masses, it is imperative that state level Consumer Protection Boards, University Grants Commission and some other leading consumer organisations are set up, with apex board at the centre, so that all sections of the society including literate and illiterate ones are made aware about the protection that consumer movement ensures. He emphasised that students had to be exposed to the acts/laws protecting the consumers in their day-to-day life, making them aware as to how to utilise the legal provisions to their advantage, where to file and how to file application or complaint and thus be able to take up their own cases in the consumer court. R. K. Murti writes in the *Hindustan Times* that though CPA provides the consumers strong weapon to protect themselves, only a microscopic minority of consumers really makes use of its provisions to strike at vested interests.

The role of mass media is important in increasing consumer awareness. Till about the 80s, rarely ever did one come across public grievances about quality of goods or services in the media. However, during the last ten years or so, the media has started taking a deep interest in the complaints of the consumer. Many newspapers run columns on specified days, through which the consumers can ventilate their grievances. Though the Indian television has launched some programmes, one being *Janvani*, and the other *Rajni*, where a consumer activist champions the cause and consumer protection programme named *Soojh Boojh.* etc. but it has not shown as much interest as it should have in protecting the interests of the consumers because of lack of funds to take their cause to the public through visual media, observes Minu in the *Hindustan Times.*

It is imperative that consumers be made aware of their rights. In such a situation media can play a very effective role in educating the masses. Media strategies be evolved in such a manner that consumers may not run after the spurious products madly which might endanger the nation building activities of a country.

Educational Development

Education is an instrument of social transformation and a change agent. It is an important input in development effort. Explaining the relevance of education in national development, the Kothari Commission observed : In a world based on science and technology, it is education that determines the level of prosperity, welfare and security of the people.

Problems of nation building are plenty and far too many. Eradication of poverty, provision of employment, national integration, strengthening democracy, bringing awareness and awakening among the people are but a few of these. Education is one of the main instruments to solve these problems and to realise expectations of the people.

As the country moves towards progress, the importance of education becomes crucial. In developing countries the emphasis is on basic education including literacy. Since this is vital to their progress, it is not only an important input for economic growth but is also a necessary element in participatory democracy. In developed countries, the infrastructure and systems to assume basic education are already in place. Their focus is, therefore, on higher and continuing education. In both categories of countries, there is growing recognition about the critical role of education. In recent years, major international agencies, too have accorded priority to education—UNDP through its Human Development Reports and of late, the World Bank. Trained manpower throughout the world and more so in societies, is becoming a precious resource. With the growing criticism of the centres of training and education, the universities in most of the countries are in the danger of becoming redundant and insignificant, as they cater to the privileged few. The recent trend towards free market economy has also made more and more countries realize the need for providing an easy access to affordable higher education to th masses.

In developing economies like India, with its growing population and aspir ations, where the resources allocated for education cater to a wide spectrum from providing basic primary education to vocational education, non-formal education, adult education and where higher education forms only one component, the liberalization has not dawned too soon.

According to Kulandaiswamy (1993), backwardness, economic or social, has unfortunately inherent in it a perpetuating potential. Countries that are underdeveloped have difficulties in liberating themselves from such a state of existence. Nevertheless their only salvation lies in empowering people with knowledge.

Whereas conventional higher education institutions, as they by and large serve the purpose, there is a need to replace it and transform into a new system where everybody regardless of sex, culture, age, social status, geographic location, linguistic barriers can have access to quality higher education to meet contemporary social needs and demands. Now this can also be an ideal recipe for a vast country like India with its own characteristic circumstances.

Conventional system of education is not cost effective. It is elitist in nature, in the sense that it is accessible only to upper and middle classes of society. The syllabus is often outdated and therefore of little relevance in today's world. Expansion through conventional means is slow and unable to meet the expectations and needs. In short, it is institution and rule centered education. The learning process of each and every student has to be tailored as per the requirement of the institution. The very purpose of education could be defeated this way.

It was under these compulsions that the Open University and the distance education system was born (Kulandaiswamy, 1993). Distance education today has come to be accepted as well recognized as a mode of education relevant to and necessary for meeting the emerging demands of the day. The emergence of science and technology as a dominant force, not only in economic development, but in human affairs in general and the dawn of the knowledge, etc. as many choose to call the present period, have brought education into the centre stage as never before in human history.

While distance education as a system in itself could be called rather young, only around 25 years old, it is blooming not only in Asia, but also in Western Europe, United States and Canada. As per the studies conducted by the NIMME of Japan in the Asia and Pacific region; and by ICDO of Open University, UK in Africa and Latin America for UNESCO, distance education is a much needed system for continuing education in the third world countries. As these countries are striving for development and new technologies are being inducted into their society, the need to catch up with new knowledge and upgrade skills has become essential for survival in the competition.

Prof. H. Kato, Director General, NIMME, in his keynote address, delivered at Teen Murti House on 'The Use of Communication Technologies for Distance Education in Japan', said that continuing education was a key concept in countries like Japan. Establishment of Lifelong Education Bureau in the place of earlier School Education Bureau on the recommendation of the Central Education Board was a step in the right direction for his country. This Lifelong Education Bureau had a broad framework covering not only continuing education, primary education, secondary education but also Kindergarten. The main concept was to look at human life as a continuous process of learning from birth to death.

A country like India will also benefit if it were to follow a similar rationale. Such an apex body could help streamline education system in the country and render education at every level more meaningful in the context of the nation building.

Distance education in its modern form—using electronic media and some elements of NICT—was pioneered by the Open University in the UK. Using broadcasting, audio/video tapes and contact sessions to supplement print material, it ought to provide education of a quality comparable to that of conventional universities. The appeal of the concept and its success spawned a large number of similar open universities across the world. With advances in NICT and its wider reach, the use of these technologies for distance education is growing.

The rapid obsolescence of knowledge requires individuals to make special efforts to stay up-to-date. This means that one can collect, process and disseminate information very quickly. Television and radio satisfactorily meet this criterion. Also, learning has to be at the pace and knowledge level of the viewer. This implies the use of viewer controlled technologies. This need is further accentuated by the fact that the viewer would like to learn at a time convenient to him/her. Apart from other reasons, this clearly indicates that continuing education has necessarily to be based on distance learning modes. The need for earning while learning is another factor that is bound to make distance education the preferred form of the future.

However, the use of NICT for education need not be limited to higher education alone. In fact, in developing countries, the problems and difficulties are far greater at the levels of basic literacy, primary education and school dropouts. Taking quality education to these segments of the population is a priority and NICT can play a major role.

In rural areas, in particular, and to reach dispersed learner groups, NICT is of great relevance. Continuing education and refresher courses for para-medical staff, agricultural extension workers and school teachers are examples of important groups that are dispersed in rural areas and often cut off from means of upgrading and updating their knowledge. Equally there is need for organized courses for farmers, craftsmen and entrepreneurs in rural areas, especially to help them cope with the changing environment and take advantage of new findings and opportunities. NICT can provide efficient and cost effective means for such courses.

Increasing privatization and commercialization of education is an evident trend world wide. To this technology has added a new dimension, globalization through transnational satellite broadcasts of distance education programmes. Though this is just the beginning, this trend is likely to continue. The implications and effects of this—especially for developing countries—need to be carefully examined. There are also larger issues about cultural diversity versus homogeneity that need consideration.

It is clear that the NICT is playing a major role in education and its potential use in future cannot be under-estimated. NICT plays a very important role in taking high quality education to the disadvantaged people and remote areas. These can be successful only if our media policy is in tune with development.

Rural Development

Rural development is the topmost priority of the contemporary planning process and also a matter of global concern. Most of the world's population lives in rural areas constituting the largest reservoir of human resources. Their mainstay is agriculture and allied activities. The meaning of rural development varies across societies, cultures and ecologies. It is a multifaceted problem causing serious concern, especially in developing countries at all stages of development.

The term 'Rural Development' has been defined in many ways. Leela (1975) defines rural development as 'an improvement in the living standards of the mass of low income population residing in rural areas and making the process self-sustaining'. According to Saha *et al.* (1978) it involves :

(i) *Physical development:* communication, transport, sewerage, irrigation, energy, forestry, animal conservation, environment;
(ii) *Economic development :* agriculture, business, industry;
(iii) *Social development :* education, culture, sports, political activities; and
(iv) *Health development :* nutrition, sanitation, community health, prevention of water and air pollution.

India is predominantly a rural country with more than 75 per cent of the population living in rural areas. Unfortunately, most of the poor in India live in rural areas under conditions which may also be described as 'backward'. In such a situation, any incidence of unemployment would necessarily affect the livelihood of casual and landless agricultural labourers who constitute more than half of the labour force and of marginal and small farmers. A little over one-third of the country's national income is derived from agriculture and allied activities, which absorbs about two-thirds of its working force. According to the 1991 census, out of the total population of over 900 million, the rural population accounted for 76.69 per cent, the urban figure being 23.31 per cent. The urban rural distribution pattern indicates that India continues to be mainly a rural country although her urban population has increased by nearly 50 millions during the last decade.

The concept of rural development envisages personal, social and economic growth of rural people as against the sole criterion or indicator of development as income generation and creation of material wealth which essentially gives rise to mindless and endless consumerism. The concept of rural development will actualise only if we make individuals as the focal point and view them in the context of their society, politics, administrative and infrastructural situations and agro-climatic environment, as against technology as the focal point to use as an instrument to exploit resources for increasing income and creating material wealth.

The major emphasis of development planning since the beginning of the Five Year Plans in 1952 has been to ameliorate the economic and social condition of those who constitute the poorest section of the rural segments and are living below the poverty line. However, massive investments over the years, running into several thousand crores of rupees, notwithstanding, the benefits have not percolated to the grassroots.

Rural development, in the broad sense of the term, holds key to all economic progress, industrial or agrarian, urban or rural. Rural development, according to the World Bank Rural Development Policy

Sector Study of 1975, has been conceptualised as a strategy designed to improve the economic and social life of a specific group of people—the rural poor— and involves extending the benefits of development to the poorest among those who seek a livelihood in rural areas.

A large number of schemes and programmes, notable amongst them being IRDP, DPAP, DDP, TRYSEM, NREP and FFW were launched primarily to improve the living standards of the mass of low income population.

Regarding the effect of rural development, Dutt (1990) has pointed out : Rural development has had the effect of increasing income disparities, even though by a process of trickling down it improves somewhat the standard of living of the poor, has dangerous potentials. The discontent caused thereby and by lack of social security which often accompanies income disparities, frequently manifests itself in undesirable channels such as religious fundamentalism, regional chauvinism and even secessionism.

According to Kamta Prasad (1990), the approach to rural development followed so far has been essentially bureaucratic rather than participatory. Rural development plans have been prepared at the national and state headquarters and passed on to local level offices of the government for execution. Involvement of the local people has been rather limited. Consequently, there has often been a mismatch between what the people wanted and what they got from the government. Whether it is IRDP, DPAP or any other programme, the dead uniformity which has occurred in the name of national planning has proved highly unproductive. As Sardar Tarlok Singh has pointed out, the interest at the higher level has been increasingly to get at quick numerical results which are easy to report, add up and publicise in one form or another with too little attention to the true impact on the conditions of the people.

In this eminently readable monograph, Development Theories—NGOs and Self Help Organizations, Bongartz (1993) has analysed as to what went wrong with the rural development approaches :

> Actually, the community development approach did not provide much support to self help activities at the village level. Decisions were still made in the centralized planning apparatus. The bulk of the input provided to the villages was absorbed by the better off sections of the rural communities. Existing power structures were accepted and not much was done to set up local self help organizations of the poor. Therefore, in terms of poverty alleviation or eradication of problems, not much progress could be reported.

There is also increasing recognition that past development efforts had not fully taken into account social and community needs, cultural values and capabilities as key elements in rural development programmes. However, now there is belated realization that the needs of the people should be at the core of the development process which should be driven by social and environmental concerns rather than economic considerations alone.

In the subsequent Five Year Plans, the Planning Commission observed: What matters is not the precise increase in national product that is achieved in five or ten years, but whether we can assure, within a specified time frame, a measurable increase in the welfare of the millions of the poor.

It is now accepted that rural development should mean not only an increase in the per capita GNP but greater equality in its composition. This would involve greater emphasis on social services like health, education, family welfare to the poor.

There is also renewed emphasis on people's participation in development programmes. According to Kamta Prasad (1990): Involvement of the local people in schemes of rural development is expected to result in better planning and decision making because the local people have a better awareness of their needs and preferences and fuller information on the conditions and possibilities of their areas. The local communities, with a more intimate knowledge of the inter-dependence of activities at the micro level, would be in a better position to develop integrated programmes which would avoid a duplication and produce the maximum impact with minimum cost.

Information and Communication Strategies

Many development thinkers and agencies are becoming increasingly determined that people's needs and demands are more fully understood, and wherever appropriate, integrated into wider development context. But mere identification of information needs of scientists, policy makers and planners, extension workers, rural community groups, and information/ communication problems vis-a-vis rural development, has no meaning unless it is matched by the design and development of appropriate information and communication strategies.

The main problem facing the country today, however, is not the lack of technologies and scientific discoveries needed for nation building, but converting these into production accomplishments and using them as an instrument of economic growth and social change. No doubt, projects are being implemented but the benefits remain peripheral. It becomes evident that neglected issues regarding the effectiveness of development communication are yet to be fully addressed. When this happens in a systematic way, progress cab be rapid. Unless we are able to reduce inequalities in communication and development, and the personnel engaged in rural development work—broadcasters, producers and writers are re-educated and made conscious of the needs and problems of the unprivileged, the positive gain shown in the increased GNP is meaningless.

Hence, it is imperative that an efficient and effective information infrastructure for rural development be developed and media strategies be geared to the ethos and relevance to the people for whom the development plans are intended to benefit. The basis of media strategies should highlight the localness of approach and dissemination of culturally appropriate and user friendly technology. Ramanamma (1993) has pointed out : There is a general assumption on the part of media professionals that they can disseminate a particular idea without a dialogue with the grassroot people because they consider themselves as 'specialists'. A majority of them show little or no respect for the experience and knowledge of the people—the creative potential of the peasants or slum dwellers. They fail to understand that poor people are more suited to depict the issues concerning them and present their own lives. In order to achieve participation, consultation, cooperation, and effective mobilization of people, the media system would need to assist in establishing a sense of community and would need a desire to resolve the issues concerning them.

The media strategies would succeed in creating the right kind of climate and environment for development only within the parameters and constraints which are associated with the rural population. These strategies would have to be innovative, realistic, chiselled and shaped to fine tune the aspirations of the people; and should preferably be operated by the local resource persons in tune with the sensibilities of the clientele.

The Information and Broadcasting Ministry is far from playing the role of a true communicating link within the government and between the government and the people in nation building activities. It utilizes its wide network and substantial resource to a great extent for entertainment without integrating socially relevant and useful message in entertainment itself. The vast potential of entertainment as a carrier of relevant messages is being exploited by advertising agencies and not by development agencies. *There is not an adequate policy-frame for an interface between communication and nation building and between different modes of communication. Communication has yet to emerge as an important policy instrument, integrating economic, social, educational and cultural planning.* It is more responsive to elite pressure which is turning the communication revolution into an instrument of consumerism and of a cultural counter reformation. Widening the rural urban and the elite mass hiatus, it is also taking us away from national integration.

The decline of the communication system implies the decline of the old world-view—the known meaning system and the known categories of understanding and interpreting natural and social reality. The breakdown of the conventional cultural apparatus means growing lag in the understanding of the changing natural and social universe, the lag in secularization of thought and consciousness. It means that trying to understand and solve problems of the emerging society with the categories and instincts of a bygone age, produce serious tensions and maladjustments. It frequently results in social and political disasters.

The cultural order is also in shambles. It is being exploited by new pedlars of entertainment, supplying vulgar and titillating entertainment and using it as a source of fortune for themselves.

The elite-mass relationship is undergoing a sea change in the context of growing consumerism in India, which alienates large sections of the elite from the masses. Consumerism also links them with the western affluent societies, alienating them from the national milieu.

As far as disseminating information is concerned, the communicators belonging to any category be it government, environmental groups or media must have a basic commitment to change. No communication can, however, succeed until it is backed by a programme. The policy decision relating to development be not taken only on papers but should also be followed up by strict implementation and monitoring.

One cannot enter the new social and communication order if one is not literate. "An illiterate person has hundreds of enemies epidemics, hunger, disorder and humiliation," said the Soviet Government's statement on elimination of illiteracy in 1920. Illiteracy makes one also a victim of false information and false consciousness. Therefore, the key to progress is education which alone can uplift a society. Human Development Report 1995 has laid great stress on women's education when it says that a year's schooling can increase a women's future earnings by about 15 per cent. Hence, the role of education in nation building.

The communication policy should ensure equitable distribution or access at one end and relevant and good quality software on the other. Communication administrators should explicitly state the rules of the game for software production and also orient them in favour of the masses. At the same time, the qualitative shift in the composition of the viewers and listeners is not brought about in favour of the masses then software will continue to reflect elite bias and dominance. The software should also be area specific. Such software can be generated if the national software production system is combined with regional and local production units which are more sensitive to the needs at the grassroots. Inose Hiroshi, a Japanese economist, suggests that "Software industry should be encouraged specially in developing countries which are trying to strengthen their system of higher education, as software production is very labour intensive and creates vast number of jobs and is also appropriate technology." In Hiroshi's view "the micro electronics revolutions today is of such immense historical significance that it too may transform developing countries which recognise its potentials, into advanced countries and pushes the advanced countries that refuse to heed its challenge to the brink of disaster. The specific target groups such as youth, women and other disadvantaged groups should be given special attention. Well designed and tested training packages should be prepared to encourage these groups to participate in the process of development.

The communication planners must consider the socio-economic implications of media policy. They must take a prominent role, both in the agenda-setting process and in devising incentive based strategies to achieve national communication goals. Communication must be tapped for promoting national development based on social justice and for enriching the quality of human life. This can be done only if it is oriented to our national genius and social milieu, if it is consciously turned to the needs and aspirations for a new life of the masses; and if communicators also learn to neutralise strong pressures and resistance from vested interests. They can play a major role in promoting development and in exercising pressure for humanising the development processes.

Gandhi called upon scientists and technologists to innovate new technologies suited to Indian condition and to the needs of the masses. His underlying concern was to avoid being imitative in the choice or transfer of technology but to be critical and innovative. According to Negrine and Papatha Nassopoulos (1991), encouraging local production and co-production are two ways to avoid being overwhelmed by imported video programmes brought in by the new media.

The global network of the present information and communication system is by and large a function of global economic arrangements. But globalisation on individual nations is being debated. According to Suprio Ghosh (1995) some scholars who adopt a critical perspective call this "cultural imperialism" or "media imperialism" of US domination of global communications. Other scholars who subscribe to "global pluralism" point out that developing countries too have become production centres of film and to programmes which they now export. They argue that satellite communication has now made decentralized production more flexible and this has led to the decline of US hegemony in communications. In a global context the tide of technology cannot be stemmed and governments have to gear themselves to maximize the benefits for human welfare through education and be able to retain their cultural identity.

Mahatma Gandhi once said,"I want the cultures of all lands to blow as freely as possible in India. But I refuse to be swept off my feet by any of them."

Hence, the overall impact of the global media on nation building can rightfully be described as a mixed bag—the greater part being filled with evils.

REFERENCES

Anand, Anita (1995). Crimes on women make news only in a scandal, *Times of India*, July 15.

Asahi Glass Foundation—*Asian Mass Communication Bulletin*, January-February, 1995-Singapore.

Bahuguna, Sunder Lal (1994). Save Gangotri in Save Himalayas; Chipko Information Centre, Silyara, Tihri Garhwal, India, p. 20, Ibid: Development Redefined, p. 38.

Bongartz, Heinz (1993). Development Theories. NGOs and Self Help Organisations. Nepal Foundation for Advanced Studies, Kathmandu, p. 6.

Distance Education Programmes in the Asia-Pacific region are covered in *Distance Education in Asia and the Pacific* (2 volumes). Asian Development Bank, Philippines, 1987. Also see *Distance Education in SAARC Countries* (ed.) Guha Biswas, National Open School, New Delhi, 1994.

Dutt, R. C. (1990). Rural Development: Some Reflections. *Yojana*, **34** (14 & 15): pp.5-8.

Ghosh, Suprio (1995). Globalising Media. *The Tribune*, May 7.

Goulet, Denis, A. (1971). *The Cruel Choice: A New Concept in the Theory of Development*, Ist edition, New York, Atheneum.

Gupta, Rahul (1994). Environment in Syllabus. The Green Book. *Financial Express*, 23 October.

Hari Jaisingh (1995). Keynote Address in the Seminar on 'Gender concerns in Mainstream Media, Beijing and Beyond, Chandigarh, June 24.

Human Development Report (1995). Unjust to Women, editorial in *Indian Express*, August 21, 1995.

Joshi, P. C. (1985). Communication and Nation Building. Sardar Patel Memorial Lectures, 1985. A Publications Division, New Delhi.

Kulandaiswamy, V. C. (1993). *Distance Education in the Indian Context*. IGNOU, New Delhi.

Leela, Uma (1975). *The Design of Rural Development; Lessons from America*. Baltimore : John Hopkins Press.

Murti, R. K. (1995). Consum er Rights and the Media. *The Hindustan Times*, September 15.

Prasad, Kamta (1990). People's Participation in Rural Development. *Yojana*, **34** (14 & 15): 15-20.

Ramachandran, Uma (1995). Coffee, Tea or Me? *The Tribune* (Sunday Reading), June 25.

Ramanamma, A. (1993). Participatory Approaches Towards More Effective Communication for Rural Development. In: K. Sadanandan Nair and Shirley—A White (eds.) *Perspectives on Development Communication*, New Delhi: Sage Publications.

Rogers, Everett, M. (1976). Communication and Development: The Passing of the Dominant Paradigm. *Communication Research*, **3**:121-33.

Saha *et al.* (1978). Role of Libraries in Rural Development in the Context of West Bengal. Paper Presented at Eighth IASLIC Seminar, Madras.

Todaro, Michael, P. (1977). *Economic Development in the Third World: An Introduction to Problems and Policies in a Global Perspective*, New York: Longman.

Usha Chander (1995). Distance Education and Media Technologies. In: V. S. Gupta, *Third Revolution in Indian Perspective*, New Delhi: Concept Publishing Co.

Walter Perry (1976). *For an excellent history and a first hand account of the UK Open University*. The Open University Press, U. K.

5

PRINT MEDIA POLICY

The print media in India continues to be in a state of buoyancy in terms of growth in circulation, number of general and news-interest newspapers and the number of languages in which the newspapers are published.

Enumerating the salient features of the Press in India, the 38th Annual Report of the Registrar of Newspapers for India for 1993 says :

(i) The total number of news-interest newspapers increased to 33,612 from 31,957 in 1992, an increase of 5.2 per cent.

(ii) The total circulation increased to 67,611,000 copies in 1993 from 63,667,000 copies in 1992, thereby registering an increase of 6.2 per cent.

(iii) Newspapers were published in 95 languages and dialects in the country, including 19 principal languages.

(iv) Language-wise, the Hindi Press continued to be in the lead both in number as well as in circulation.

(v) Uttar Pradesh leads in regard to the number of newspapers as well as in respect of circulation.

During 1993 newspapers were published in as many as 96 languages/dialects. Apart from English and 18 other principal languages enumerated in the Eighth Schedule of the Constitution, newspapers were published in 77 other languages mostly Indian languages or dialects and a few foreign languages. Hindi newspapers numerically constituted the largest group in the country. As in the previous years, highest number of newspapers were published in Hindi (12,596) followed by English (5,316), Urdu (2,224), Bengali (2,036), Marathi (1,561) and Tamil (1,460).

In circulation too, Hindi newspapers maintained their lead with 27,938,000 copies, followed by English with 9,010,000 copies. The third position was claimed by Malayalam press.

Some of the major policy issues confronting the print media have been—entry of foreign print media in the country, strengthening the regulatory mechanism, institution of Ombudsman and the Press Council of India. Some other questions like formulating the code of ethics in view of the controversy about financial inducements offered to and accepted by the journalists, hold of big industrial houses over newspapers, supermacy of news room vs board room also need to be articulated in the context of print media policy.

Recently, the Chairman of the Press Council of India, Justice P. B. Sawant said : Hiring of editorial staff in newspapers on contract basis, where permanent work was involved was a practice detrimental to the freedom of the Press and the matter could be taken up under the Industrial Disputes Act.

Replying to questions at a "Meet the Press" programme at Pune, Justice Sawant said that journalists could approach the State and Central Governments against the practice of hiring editorial staff on contract basis. He also considered the hold of big industrial houses over newspaper industry, the entry of politicians into the business of print media as another " grave danger" to the preservation of freedom of the Press in the country.*

Entry of Foreign Print Media

An issue which has polarised the media community, overheated the debate on the subject, with both the protagonists and the opponents speaking on the move with almost religious fervour. The opinion amongst the members of the Council of Ministers seems to be divided. Those favouring the move consider the step as the logical outcome of the on-going process of liberalisation, whereas those opposing advise caution against going blind folded into an unknown area and cite the 1955 cabinet decision disallowing such entry as sacrosanct.

Cultural imperialism, foreign invasion, patriotism and values under siege, access to more information, these and other cliches are doing the rounds in media circles. Our media are now-a-days facing an issue as important as the spiked defamation bill which was introduced by Rajiv Gandhi. The only difference is that at that time the media were one and now they are dispersed. The possibility of entry of the foreign press has raised the hackles of not only the politicians but also some journalists. The issue has been raised in the Parliament, taken before the judiciary and has been the subject of passionate and heated debate in the columns of the press.

---

*The Hindustan Times, 11 October 1995.

The raging debate over the issue has divided the media as well as the politicians into warring camps. One group feels that the foreigners are coming here only for ravaging our five thousand year old culture and traditions. They are the evil incarnate who are all set to subvert our social and secular fabric. Now, their eyes are set to stop us from our onward march ahead. Gaining entry into India is an excuse for the cultural imperialism of the country. Profit may not be the only criterion for the press coming to India. These can very well be propaganda and power. Many European countries do not allow the foreign press to operate from their soil, so why should we ?

The second point is that no one is powerful enough to destroy our deep-rooted and ancient tradition. Are we so weak or our culture so fragile that it can be plundered so easily ? Moreover, if the foreign media come they will bring better and newer technology resulting in superior publications for the consumers to choose from. The foreign media have no axe to grind and are here only for the purpose of expanding their business. They will create more job opportunities for Indian journalists. The foreign media cannot operate on their ground rules but have to function within the periphery of the rules laid down by the government. Thus, these are incapable of subverting our national interest.

The reality is that both sides are motivated by mercantile gains. Protagonists of the move say that the opponents use the facade of patriotism and culture to save their media interests, since they are dishing out mediocrity and shoddiness, they feel threatened of competition. Moreover, foreign newspapers and magazines are allowed in the country without any import duties which shows that we are not unknown to the views of the foreign press. In fact, India has a chance of becoming the media and the information centre of the entire South Asian region. The foreign press can do a lot to improve our depleted image abroad. Recent trends show that the information industry is fast on its way to becoming the largest industry in the world. Foreign press is going to bring in competition and newer technology which will go a long way in providing a choice to the consumers.

The opponents of this move say that already foreign television has cast a detrimental effect on the younger generation who are being swayed by a culture alien to us. Moreover, we do not need competition as we have more than enough of internal competition. The entry of foreign media is going to affect the small and the vernacular press and not the English language press. Our ethos and culture are such that we live in the environs of compassion and not cut throat competition. Such a condition is not congenial for our interests and culture.

In an impassioned article : Foreign media inside the Indian fourth estate* V. R. Krishna Iyer, says : To commoditise the media and allow their foreign manufacture within the country is fraught with grave risk to our sovereign democracy and nationalist survival. After all, freedom of the press is but a derivative from the fundamental freedom of expression under Article 19. Freedom of speech and of occupation or business belong only to the Indian citizens and are subject to reasonable restrictions " in the interests of sovereignty and integrity of India .... friendly relations with foreign states, public order, decency or morality or in relation to contempt of court, defamation or incitement to an offence." No 'open sesame' for an outside news heavy weight can be mindlessly granted. He further adds : There is nothing in national life which cannot be shaken or shaped by alien agencies once they get a foothold. To caricature or debunk Indian events and developments and make the world outside hostile to us is an easy process once the foreign barons are in. Moreover, a tremendous expansion of information and communication with its manipulable effects, makes the culture and conscience of our people a victim of the foreign media. Their commercial conquest of our economy and their influence on people's tastes and interests and values are so complete that the excesses in which they indulge for control of the minds and markets makes one tremble.

The Interaction on, Entry of Foreign News Papers in India, organised by the National Media Centre on 25 September 1994, brought out salient features of the issue in terms of plurality of views, range and presentation of opinion.

The former Minister for Information and Broadcasting P. Upendra was of the opinion that compared to the advantages, the entry of foreign media would pose more disadvantages, "Probably, we cannot control the motivated presentation of news, with their editorial set up here. And the restraint which the Indian newspapers generally exercise in case of some sensitive issues like communal clashes, caste wars, etc. probably you may not expect the same treatment from the foreign papers. Here we are guided by the Indian law. After all, you know, news presentations differ from paper to paper even today in India. I do not think that kind of restraint can be exercised by the foreign papers. And more and more sensationalism and yellow journalism is likely to come because we have been seeing this in very top newspapers abroad ... Front pages are full of stories like rapes, murders and robberies rather than some important news. And competition will come into that field and probably our papers will be forced to follow suit to compete. This kind of thing will come. Therefore, my personal

**Times of India*, 29 October 1994.

feeling is : the disadvantages are many compared to a few advantages which may come. What we can do is : *The Herald Tribune* case has been mentioned. *USA Today* is there. Perhaps you can start with allowing the satellite printing of certain newspapers without any editorial set-up in this country. They can be allowed because even if you do not allow here, they may start in Nepal or they can start in Sri Lanka and still circulate it in India. You cannot prevent such a kind of situation. If somebody wants to have printing facility to have satellite editions, probably he can do that. At a certain stage, you can allow."

Finally, he suggested that in such a serious matter, which would affect the entire media scene in the country, it should not be left to the government alone to immediately take a decision. A high level committee should be appointed with some government representatives, some media experts, some journalists unions, etc. to go into this problem in depth and give a report. Ultimately, this must be discussed in Parliament before the government takes a final decision.

In another interesting presentation, T. N. Ninan, who very articulately spoke for the entry of foreign print media side : Information in on way to becoming the world's largest industry. It will be bigger than the manufacturing of steel or cars and information highways are going to encircle the globe. Technology forces its own changes. Computer technology is converging with telecommunications technology and both are getting together with the information industry. You can soon get video signals on the same optical fibre lines to connect your telephone. You can have data in many forms on the same set of lines. Technology today covers telephones, fax machines, computers, photocopiers and T.V. screens. You get fax newspapers already being faxed from overseas into hotel rooms in India every morning.

He also referred to the Khyber Pass mentality—that we are going to be invaded. That Khyber Pass could be used to reach out to the world. It has, however, been generally agreed that before any policy decision is taken by the government, there has to be a frank discussion and national debate so that views of the press, political parties and people in public life are available for a national consensus.

Changing Values in Journalism

During the past few years, and more so in the recent past, the lowering ethical values in the media have been widely reported. The pernicious practice of accepting envelopes containing gift coupons or hard cash by the press reporters in India at the press conferences where new issues are launched has been widely commented upon. Writing in *The Tribune* 'Strange Results of Liberalisation', one of the eminent columnists M.V. Kamath says : What journalists should be concerned about is the corruption of their brethren on a scale that is mind boggling. Giving a graphic account of the process of cash collection in a day in the life of a reporter, Kamath also points to another aspect of the problem -— Conformity. "Does that mean there are no honest journalists in the profession. The issue is not honesty but conformity. If the honest journalist refuses to accept the gifts given to him he falls foul of his colleagues. Every one accepts gifts. That is done thing."

Writing of Business Journalists in *Vidura* (July 1995), Nandini Sahai says : Then there is another class of journalists who are not doing too badly. They call themselves "business journalists", whose primary function is to attend press conferences, specially those aimed at announcing share-issues. They stand to take home quite a neat sum at the end of the month, mostly in the form of gift coupons and gifts. *The Vidura* issue of June 1994, has Mr. Dilip Cherian saying, "My own personal experience is that in business journalism the chances of becoming corrupt are much higher." It has also succeeded in creating a breed of journalists who boldly "offer to pay" the newspaper for the privilege of being their "financial correspondent." This was the experience of Mr. Kamath as he related it in *The Tribune* of June 11. He says he was in Bombay last February to interview candidates for a financial correspondent's position with *The Statesman*. The response, as might have been expected, was good. But there was one candidate who was uninterested in what *The Statesman* could offer; on the contrary he was prepared to pay them a monthly sum for the privilege of being their financial correspondent!

Not that the phenomenon of journalists getting rich in the course of news gathering is peculiar to India. In China, a lot of Chinese journalists "write advertisements in the guise of news after receiving various benefits". In April 1994, the Chinese Communist Party launched a drive to root out the spreading phenomenon of paid news coverage (cheque book journalism) in the country's media organs. A circular put out by the Central Committee's propaganda department called for, "unremitting efforts by party organisations to educate journalists on press ethics."

Captioned as 'China cracks down on chequebook journalism,' the above report carried by the *Times of India*, 27 April 1994, referred to the standard package followed by journalists in covering promotional events which include a small gift, a red paper bag with cash and a banquet after a press conference. The circular further noted : Some correspondents had seriously disrupted the economic order and harmed the interests of the state and people by taking news stories in favour of the sponsoring parties, it said. The practice of demanding and accepting favours for news coverage reached its climax in 1992. A few reporters could not be attracted to a press conference if they were unable to receive... benefits. Some crew members from television stations went even further. The officials of Chinese television organisations are known to ask for thousands of U.S. dollars in return for arranging "interviews" with no promise that the deal would be carried out. Making a presentation on the question of ethics and values and media in one of the seminars held in Bangalore recently, the Dean of the Asian School of Journalism said: There is also a need to look into financial inducements that are offered to newsmen by political parties and companies. The small fortunes paid by Mulayam Singh Yadav to newsmen in Uttar Pradesh indicate how deep this malaise has spread. Sums amounting from 10 to 15 lakhs were disbursed by Mulayam Singh to turn the press pliant.

Similarly, a fiscal ceiling needs to be arrived at regarding the gifts that companies disburse to newsmen. Should they be limited to calendars or diaries? Or should they include products like watches or suitlengths? How far can one go in accepting such freebies–a free trip, a free lunch. Or may be more? This is a grave ethical question again, and needs to be attended to if doubts have to be removed from people's minds regarding the integrity of the media.

He suggested that a code of ethics needs to be formulated by media men which should be displayed in the reporter's room and on the newsdesk. It should also be published once a year in all newspapers so that readers know the ethical standards to which newspapers subscribe. The Note on National Media Policy, issued as a Discussion Paper, by the Ministry of Information and Broadcasting, also points out that the press should repudiate the extension of any direct financial assistance or subsidy, in the form of release of government advertisements, etc. that may ultimately dilute the freedom. The Note also wants that the government must seriously consider withdrawing the facility of provision of residential accommodation, etc.

Reporting Communal Issues in the Language Press

Journalism in vernacular languages in India and several other countries has encouraged linguistic, ethnic and sectarian passions and worked to the advantage of fissiparous tendencies. Vernacular newspapers focus on fostering religious and communal divisiveness, emphasize casteism and negative aspects of the news.

As a legacy from the preparation days, when in India more than the English language press, the vernacular press was responsible for aggravating the communal situation, the situation today is no better. At that time the Marathi press of Bombay and Pune conducted equally provocative campaign against partition. The Marathi press made biting attacks on the weaknesses of the Congress policy of *de-Hinduising* the country and rejected and ridiculed the Congress appeals for moderation as attempts to escape criticism.

With competing public and political interests, reporting communal riots has always been a complex task—it has become all the more acute in recent times. There have been instances of deliberate and reckless spread of falsehood where media reportage has exacerbated conflict in which interest of the nation as such have suffered. Sadly it is the later which has become more common in significant sections of the press in recent years.

While censoring four leading Hindi dailies, the Press Council of India in its findings in January 1991 in the Ayodha case said: *Gross irresponsibility and impropriety offending the cannons of journalistic ethics to promote mass hysteria on the basis of rumours and speculation.* One paper carried the report: "Muslim doctors of Aligarh Muslim University Hospital are deliberately killing Hindu patients." This report was also brought to the notice of Press Council of India. In this context the widely read columnist, S. Nihal Singh said : This was a national crisis with passions at fever pitch over an issue that had a deep and painful past and a disturbing present in the form of recurring Hindu Muslim riots. How did the press report the crisis? Let us first look at the major newspapers in Hindi and Urdu. They were, as a rule, totally partisan. Much of the reporting on either side was tendentious, some of it highly exaggerated and it seemed that protagonists on each side were only too eager to fan the flames of the communal fire. Some of these erring newspapers later won the rebuke of the Press Council of India. Most of the English newspapers behaved responsibly although in some cases, the stories seemed to be coloured to some extent by their reporters' religion.

In the related context of reporting Indo-Pakistan affairs also the regional press has been far from moderate and objective. In a seminar on, 'Role of Media in a National Crisis' organised by AMIC Fazal Qureshi, Managing Director and the Chief Editor of the Pakistani Press International News Agency said: The national press failed to play the moderating role which it should always play in the larger interests of regional peace and harmony. It is not only the Pakistan press which deserves criticism on this account. The press in India and Pakistan, with notable exceptions, have always failed to play their role as peacemaker. A look at the Indian and Pakistani newspapers will tell a similar story. Pakistan newspapers freely sensationalize the actions of the Indian army in Kashmir and the Punjab. In the Indian newspapers, exaggerated accounts of Pakistani infiltrators and saboteurs helping the secessionists in Punjab and Kashmir get the same kind of prominent display. In reply Pakistani newspapers blame Indian agents for the law and order situation in Sind. The general reporting trend in both countries is to pick and play up the negative and darker side of the picture. The press in the two countries, along with politicians and governments, can be accused of continuing to poison the atmosphere between the two neighbours. It is time we realize the dangers of such action, which is not in the interest of the two countries. The events in Kashmir, Punjab and Sind are most unfortunate and the press cannot black out news of events. However, the press should try to act more sensibly, more soberly and more maturely, pleading for sanity on all sides in its news, editorials and commentaries. It should build up public opinion against use of force and put its full weight behind solutions by dialogue.

Regional Press

The doyen of Indian journalists, the late M.Chalapathi Rau Wrote: The future of the Indian press means essentially the future of the Indian language press. India will have gradually mammoth circulation in all the Indian languages.

There is no doubt that with increase in literacy and in the purchasing power of the people living in slums in the cities, and in the rural areas, there will be significant increase in the circulation of regional language newspapers, not only in India, but in Asia as a whole. In a futuristic study on the development of the press in the year 2000, it has been stated that the present public policy against the growth of a monopoly press and in favour of small and medium sized newspapers is likely to continue. The vast size of the country, multiplicity of languages and cultures, and the varying types of regional and local problems also favour the growth of the small and medium sized regional press. With regional development and growth of democratic institutions, a number of newspapers, primarily for the consumption of the literate masses in the rural areas, may also be published. The experience of European countries where the number of newspapers has declined and the concentration of newspapers in the hands of a few groups has increased, is not likely to be manifest in India. Small and medium sized local newspapers will predominate in the country, but despite their predominance, the big papers published from metropolitan and large cities will share a greater proportion of the total newspaper circulation.

In the context of the predominance of small and medium sized newspapers, it will be pertinent to underline the importance of rural press. Rural press serves the function of reinforcing literacy or preventing readers from lapsing into illiteracy once again, as a medium of community communication and as a link between the policy makers, development bureaucracy and farmers. Wilbur Schramm, in his book, Mass Media and National Development, considered rural newspapers as one of the great movers of national development.

At a time when the government has, once again, embarked upon the policy of encouraging and strengthening *Panchayati Raj* institutions in the country, the following observations made in Mass Media and National Development, a media classic by Wilbur Schramm (1964) are quite relevant.

> Sometimes it has been asked whether the host of small district newspapers which have come out in recent years serve any useful purpose. They are said to confine their attention mainly to local complaints and disputes. I have regarded these district papers as of immense value, for they focus the attention of the local population on local development effort and assist in creating interest in the local affairs. I personally know of a number of cases in which these small newspapers have exercised considerable influence on local administration and have helped to build local opinion on political and economic issues. If development requires local participation, these district papers have to play an important role in mobilizing local effort. It may be conceded that all of them are not motivated by the highest ideals, and some of them may be instruments of local politicians, but as a whole they are of great assistance to local development. Political decentralization and establishment of *Panchayati Raj* have created a new political structure in local administration. The zila parishads and panchayat samitis have been entrusted with wide powers in the spheres of local administration and local development. The small district newspapers have the same significance in local affairs as provincial papers in state matters and metropolitan papers in national problems. The study team on Five Year Plan publicity has described this section of the press as the most important link in the communication chain. There can be little doubt of what a healthy mofussil press can do to inculcate high ideals of public service and a sense of dedication to people's weal and welfare in the making of the local self-governing institutions.

Apart from the important print media policy issues discussed in this chapter—Entry of the Foreign Print Media, Changing Values in Journalism and Declining Ethical Standards, Reporting Communal Issues in the Language Press, and role of Regional and Community Press, it would be equally important to refer to regulatory mechanism for the print media—Press Council of India. The guidelines laid down by the Council for reporting communal events have been reproduced in the annexures. The Council figures in greater detail in the chapter on Regulatory Measures and Watchdog Mechanism.

REFERENCES

Bhatti, Razia (1995). The influence of policies and government on communication ethics. *Media Asia* **22** (1): 3-8.

John, L. (1976). The Messenger's Motives ..... Ethical Problems of News Media. Prentice Hall, Inc., New Jersey.

Press Institute of India (1995). Journalists for Sale. *Vidura* **32** (2): 10-12.

Nihal Singh, S. (1992). *Your Slip is Showing–Indian Press Today.* UBS Publishing, New Delhi.

Nihal Singh, S. (1993). Painful Splits. In : *Role of Media in a National Crisis.* AMIC, Singapore, pp.19-26.

Qureshi, Fazal (1993). Serving the Nation. In : *Role of Media in a National Crisis.* AMIC, Singapore, pp. 69-76.

6

ELECTRONIC MEDIA POLICY

The pervasive character of electronic media–radio, television and cable television—in terms of sweep, socio-cultural impact, capacity to influence the contemporary values of the audience and the viewers has confronted the policy makers, society and planners with a host of issues. Some of these issues have been with us for over more than two decades now–autonomy of electronic media, credibility of the news programmes put out by the government controlled segment. The yawning gap between the precepts and practice—codes and guidelines notwithstanding, has also been a subject of recurring comments by the media analysis.

A discussion on electronic media policy would inevitably take us to a number of reports of the Working Groups, the legislation enacted by the government particularly the Prasar Bharati Act, 1990 and the Cable Television Network Act, 1995, besides the landmark judgement of the Supreme Court declaring airwaves as the public property and asking the government to constitute an independent, autonomous public authority. The reports, codes and guidelines, legislation and the Supreme Court Judgement have generated voluminous literature on almost all aspects of the working of electronic media.

Television Expansion in India—Policy Initiatives

The television world today is changing rapidly and fast. During the last five years forces of change have gathered greater momentum. The expansion of television—in terms of number of TV sets, both colour and black and white, number of transmitters and Programme Production Centres, number of channels, types of programmes including introduction of Movie Channel from 7 April 1995, has led to the exponential growth of the medium. The two references given below briefly recapitulate the television scenario in the country.

Television is poised for a boom in India and other adjoining Asian countries, which will radically alter consumption patterns in the region, according to Merrill Lynch, the world-renowned securities and economics research firm. It has also predicted that the media could usher in fundamental social, economic and political changes in the region.

— Merrill Lynch sees TV boom in India,
Times of India, 20 October, 1994.

Interestingly, in this age of colour, the near outdated black and white TV is staging a come back. Its resurgence has been largely possible due to an increase in demand from a sector that was unthinkable five years back. Today it is the *jhuggi* dweller, who in the largest buyer. The new buyer is clearly demarcated and comes from three distinct backgrounds. First is the *jhuggi* dweller, a close second is the middle class family that wants to buy a second TV for their homes and the third is the shopkeeper, who wants to be entertained at his shop. With an increase in the number of channels following the satellite invasion, the concept of portable black and white as a second TV is coming in a big way in middle class homes. The youngsters want to watch programmes of their choice and not what their parents prefer.

— Boom in sale of portable black & white TVs,
Indian Express, 7 March 1995.

The rapid television proliferation—an ongoing process since 1984—is gathering speed in the wake of cable and satellite television invasion. Television in India is no longer an urban phenomenon. It is fast penetrating into mofussil and rural areas of the country. The major satellite and cable television companies in the world view India as one of the top five TV markets in the 21st century. And now with the Supreme Court Judgement on freeing the airwaves from governmental monopoly, and private broadcasters, TV programme is poised to break new grounds in a big way as never before.

Alongwith this rapid and unchartered expansion of television in India are tied a host of related socio–cultural issues–cultural alienation, accessibility, credibility, violence and vulgarity, encouragement to the forces of commercialisation and consumerism in the society. Equally important are the regulatory aspects and role of media watchdogs; codes and norms evolved to regulate broadcasting; all these have been major concerns for quite some time. In terms of comments, reviews and critiques, no other medium–print, radio, cinema—caught the fancy of the analysts as television has.

Television was introduced in India as an experimental pilot project to study its use, 'as a medium of education, rural uplift and community development.' This experimental service was inaugurated by the President on 15 September 1959, heralding the use of the medium for special educational programmes: adult and health education, promotion of recreational community activities and in a limited way, to supplement school education.

The introduction of television in India was a major policy initiative, planned under the inspiration and guidance of Dr. Vikram Sarabhai who envisioned the possibility of using television as a method of spreading education, leap frogging from the state of economic backwardness and social disabilities in decades rather than centuries. The pioneering efforts of Dr. Sarabhai and Dr. M. S. Swaminathan resulted in the launching of Krishi Darshan Programme, for the popularisation of improved agricultural practices from 26 January 1967.

The pace of television expansion in the initial years has been haphazard and uneven. It was initially assigned low priority, and hence there was hardly any expansion till October 1972, when the Television Centre at Bombay was launched.

During the first decade of its growth (1959-69) television was confined to the national capital. During the second decade (1969-79), apart from three metropolitan cities—Bombay, Calcutta and Madras, it was introduced in a few urban centres and some rural areas. The two significant developments during the second decade were : separation of the TV from All India Radio and introduction of commercials, both in 1976. Television became an independent media unit in the Ministry of Information and Broadcasting under the banner—Doordarshan.

It was only in 1982—the year of the Asiad— when it was decided to switch over to colour transmission. In July 1983 the government approved the Special Plan for the expansion of the television network. With the operationalisation of the Indian National Satellite INSAT-IB, 126 transmitters were added to achieve the coverage of 70 per cent of the population. During this period television expansion leap frogged so much so that during 1984 for several months, the effort of the government was to commission one relay station per day. One important and far reaching effect of this rapid hardware expansion was, as pointed out by media analyst Bella Mody, that aspects of education and development in programming began to get slowly marginalised. This pattern of television introduction, early public service rhetoric, educational implementation and then implementation on a large scale for elite pacification would repeat itself in India.

The eighties witnessed a great leap forward in the growth of television, in terms of reach, area of activities and the number of TV sets in the country. Programmes for entertainment have been many— film songs sequence, feature films, soap operas like *Humlog* and *Yeh Jo Hai Zindgi*, two famous epics– *Ramayana* and *Mahabharta*, hooked the viewers as never before. The scenario became vibrant and colourful— both literary and figuratively; tele-actors and actresses became house–hold names as also the comperes and news-readers—atleast the popular ones. Television was no longer an elitist medium—confined to only the exclusive sections of the society. There were occasions — particularly during the period when the two popular epic serials were being screened — when social engagements and public fixtures were tailored according to TV programmes. These programmes contributed to the society becoming TV conscious.

Establishment of Working Groups

The discussion on electronic media policy has been greatly enriched by the deliberations, reports and recommendations of several committees constituted by the government during the last more than 25 years. These Committees and Working Groups, comprising eminent experts and leading professionals provided precious inputs and guidelines on a wide range of issues. The mandate given to several of these committees was to examine and evaluate policies and programmes of media organisations; recommend autonomy for Akashvani and Doordarshan and software plan for Doordarshan. The evaluation reports of the SITE, Reports and Papers on Mass Communication by UNESCO and the Report of the International Commission for the Study of Communication Problems constituted by UNESCO in 1977 also contributed a large body of information, covering the widest possible spectrum and different perspectives on issues impinging upon communication and development. Salient features of reports and recommendations of some of the committees and projects, which have a vital bearing on policy issues, are enumerated briefly as under:

The Committee on Broadcasting and Information Media (1964), also known as the Chanda Committee, constituted in December 1964 presented the Report on Radio and Television in April 1966. The Committee observed : It is not possible in the Indian context for a creative medium like broadcasting to flourish under a regiment (sic) of departmental rules and regulations. It is only by an institutional change that AIR can be liberated from the present rigid financial and administrative procedures of the government. It recommended that the separate corporations be set up for Akashvani and Doordarshan which should have the freedom to evolve its own methods of recruitment, regulated scales of pay and conditions of service according to its needs, and devise a financial and accounting system appropriate to its creative activity.

This recommendation was considered by the Cabinet in December 1969 and the Lok Sabha was informed in April 1970 that the present was not an opportune time to consider the conversion of All India Radio into an autonomous Corporation. However, another important recommendation that Akashvani and Doordarshan be separated was accepted and took effect from 1 April 1976.

Arguing for the grant of autonomy to the two media the Committee said: Theoretically it (AIR) has the freedom of a national newspaper to present objectively topics of current interest but in practice it has failed to do so mainly for two reasons. First, successive ministers usurped the policy making functions of the Director General and started interfering even in matters of programme planning and presentation, and second, the selection of the directing staff was so made as to ensure unquestioning compliance. As a result the public image of AIR has become tarnished, its objectivity destroyed and its initiative gradually whittled away.

The SITE, one year pilot project in 1975-76, was primarily undertaken to experiment with television through satellite communication to broadcast special programmes in six states which included 2400 villages. The Experiment aroused wide international interest. India was the only developing country in the region to undertake an experiment using space age technology to bring its millions into the mainstream of national life, make them aware of the changing pattern of present day urban life and help them to harness their resources for optimum benefits. Explaining the importance of SITE, Narayana Menon (1976), in his book, *The Communication Revolution* wrote:

> SITE means a lot of things apart from being an experiment. For one thing, it made India TV-conscious—and of an advanced style of TV technology. TV is no more confined to the main metropolitan centres. It has suddenly made its presence felt in the villages of Karnataka, Andhra, Orissa, Madhya Pradesh, Bihar, Rajasthan. Hundreds of engineers, technicians, mechanics are acquiring new skills and vast experience. Programmers and broadcasters and telecasters are getting new insights into the medium. In spite of all the doubts and hesitations, bureaucratic stumbling blocks, genteel

infighting, shortage of equipment, facilities, money, we were in the middle of a vast learning process, the culmination of the tentative approaches of the tele-club days of 1959. All these things add up to substantial investments which should, in the long run, bring rich dividends. As Vikram Sarabhai said, television is an investment rather than an overhead.

However, the former Director–General of Akashvani, P. C. Chatterjee, while commenting on the achievements of SITE observed : In the practical aspects of nation building on which programmes were telecast during SITE, i.e. agriculture, animal husbandry, health and nutrition, family planning and in telecasts for schools, we find that the gains were rather meagre.

The Working Group on Autonomy for Akashvani and Doordarshan (1977), also known as Verghese Committee, appointed in August 1977, submitted its Report in February 1978. The Report is a landmark document on the aspect of granting autonomy to the electronic media. Its major recommendations were :

(i) An autonomous National Broadcast Trust should be established under which Akashvani and Doordarshan would function. It gave a name to the proposed authority—Akash Bharati : The National Broadcast Trust;

(ii) Radio and TV should work for the public purpose. They should function within the framework of a broad perspective of national communication policy;

(iii) The proposed autonomous broadcasting trust authority should be owned by the nation and be accountable to the Parliament;

(iv) The priority of broadcasting has to change from urban–elitist moorings to the rural and semi-urban areas and to the urban poor. The quality of programmes would have to improve. It should also work towards filling the rural-urban and tradition –modernity gaps;

(v) The idea of one autonomous corporation each for All India Radio and Doordarshan did not find support from the Working Group. It opted for one autonomous National Trust for both of the broadcast media—radio and television. It also rejected the concept of autonomous regional corporations, but it envisaged decentralization of national broadcasting authority; and

(vi) The autonomy of the authority and independence from control of the government should be guaranteed by the Constitution.

The government later on introduced the Prasar Bharati (Broadcasting Corporation of India) Act in September 1990. The continued foot dragging on the implementation of the Prasar Bharati Act and the yawning gap between the government's rhetoric and its practice has confined the implementation of the issue of autonomy for the electronic media to a dream as distant as ever.

The International Commission for the Study of Communication Problems (1977) was established by UNESCO, to study, among other issues such as increasing importance attached to communication as a social phenomenon and the consequent interest shown in the development of communication media; the growing impact and repercussions of technological progress in the field, etc. The President of the Commission, Sean MacBride, transmitted the Final Report to the Director General, UNESCO in February 1980. Some of the important recommendations of the Commission are :

(i) Communication be no longer regarded merely as an incidental service and its development left to chance. Recognition of its potential warrants the formulation by all nations, and particularly developing countries, of comprehensive communication policies linked to overall social, cultural, economic and political goals. Such policies should be based on inter-ministerial and inter-disciplinary consultations with broad public participation;

(ii) Within the framework of national development policies, each country will have to work out its own set of priorities, bearing in mind that it will not be possible to move in all directions at the same time. But, as far as resources allow communication policies should aim at stimulating and encouraging all means of communication;

(iii) The communication component in all development projects should receive adequate financing. So-called "development support communications" are essential for mobilizing initiatives and providing information required for action in all fields of development—agriculture, health and family planning, education, religion, industry and so on. Essential communication needs to be met include the extension of basic postal services and telecommunication networks through small rural electronic exchanges; and

(iv) Development strategies should incorporate communication policies as an integral part in the diagnosis of needs and in the design and implementation of selected priorities. In this respect communication should be considered a major development resource, a vehicle to ensure real political participation in decision making, a central information base for defining policy options, and an instrument for creating awareness of national priorities.

The Working Group of Software Planning for Doordarshan (1983), also popularly known as the Joshi Committee, was established to make recommendations regarding programming in Indian television. It submitted its Report in April 1984, sub-titled, 'An Indian Personality for Television', which was formally laid on the table of Lok Sabha in 1985. Even though the Working Group was formed to make recommendations regarding Doordarshan, its Report underlines the overall communication approach and policy concerning other sectors of mass media.

The Working Group Report made several recommendations on creating appropriate environment for the development of creative software for Doordarshan. In the first place the Working Group was convinced that such an environment did not exist within the present structure of the organization. It was also convinced that whatever the claims of the government, Doordarshan did not enjoy 'functional freedom' and the lack of such freedom is having a detrimental effect on the planning and quality of its programmes.

The Working Group recommended the setting up of a National Doordarshan Council which would have three roles to perform : to review and guide the organisation's performance, as a guardian of Doordarshan's functional and professional autonomy, and as a counterpart of the Press Council for examining complaints of inaccuracy or bias in the reporting of news and comment on current affairs.

The Report emphasized that a developing country like India is exposed to the danger of erosion of its national cultural identity, and the need is to resist the cultural invasion from outside through restriction of imported programmes and 'positive software planning'. It discerned a credibility gap created by the growing hiatus between profession and practice, between official policy pronouncements emphasising use of television for development and education, and the increasing drift and departure from them in actual programming. It, therefore, urged the exploitation of the 'development potential' of television, of using communication technology for 'leap frogging into growth and development'. It endorsed and Nehru and Sarabhai approach of tapping the communication revolution in general and television in particular as a major weapon in the fight against poverty and illiteracy.

Indian Television—Policy Issues

Government Monopoly Control of Electronic Media

The most striking aspect of the electronic media scenario in the country today is the overwhelming degree of the government control under which the media operates. As outlined in the foregoing discussion above, easing government control and granting autonomy/functional autonomy has been one of the important terms of reference of several committees and Working Groups.

The government has always justified its monopoly of broadcasting on diverse grounds: (a) broadcast media must be used to educate and inform the masses, (b) it should not be allowed to be exploited by commercial interests or made use of by elements questioning the sovereignity of the country.

An other Committee, established under the Chairmanship of K. A. Varadan, in its recommendations submitted in November 1991, expressed the view that the electronic media should cease to be the exclusive state preserve. The Committee suggested that the Broadcasting Council of India as envisaged in the Prasar Bharati Act be entrusted with the functions of licensing, monitoring of programmes and quality rating. However, the recommendations of the Varadan Committee were also disregarded by the government.

Credibility and Objectivity of Programmes

The credibility and objectivity of electronic media are the two essential pre-requisites for building up values of trust and reliability between the media and its users. It is more so when the power and the reach of the electronic media has increased phenomenally, thanks to the burgeoning expansion of the television network in the country.

Notwithstanding the formulation of various guidelines and codes—the two important being, The Broadcast Code governing All India Radio and Guidelines for News Policy for Broadcast Media; the plummeting credibility of the media in the eyes of the viewers and listeners has further widened the hiatus between what is implemented in practice and what has been prescribed. Lack of concern for the concept of credibility has been too well documented to need elaboration.

In her book, *Broadcasting and the People*, Mehra Masani wrote: Suppression or dilution of news and opinions unpalatable to the government occurs from time to time, but even more common is infiltration into the bulletins of comparatively unimportant items pertaining to the government and the ruling party.

The TV news is nothing but a listing and a litany of ministerial activities and an unending catalogue of inane pronouncements of the political masters of the day. Unfortunately, however, credibility and objectivity continue to be the major casualities and the misuse of electronic media goes on unabated, codes and guidelines notwithstanding.

> Here one is reminded of the apt observations of Nani A. Palkhivala: Radio and television are not only owned by the government but unashamedly controlled by the government. The only reason why the press, with its accent on investigative journalism, is rendering such signal service to the nation—while our radio and television are boneless, spineless and gutless, and have lost all credibility—is that the former is free from the shackles of the government.

In one of its Special Reports on Doordarshan, Hijacking the Medium, *India Today* analysed the gaping hole that exists between the Precept and Practice and as to how objectivity and fairplay are sacrificed at the altar of political gain and expediency. The Special Report gives a blow by blow account of how rules and guidelines are just given a go by in an attempt to cater to the political exigencies of the ruling party. The situation has, if any, deteriorated to an extent that news bulletins and current affair programmes at the Doordarshan lack objectivity.

The result of the policy of news manipulation over the years has been that the people have, by and large, lost faith in the credibility of Akashvani and Doordarshan and are turning to foreign networks in order to get the true and correct perspective of news and events. The Indian listeners tune into news organisations like B. B. C. for authenticity and impartiality of news rather than their national broadcasting organization.

The way the government has vetoed the live news and views-related telecasts on Channel-3, and instead approved only recorded presentation of news and current affairs programmes, holds little hope of the balanced and fair news broadcasst through the electronic media. The cabinet's insistence on vetting the news before it is telecast and prior recording of panel discussions is mesant to ensure censoring of anything unacceptable to the establishment. What is regrettable is, however, the failure to realize that such an approa s ch is bound to prove counter-productive, in that when credibility is discounted, the effectiveness and impact of the exercise is lost on the viewers.

Software Planning

Concern for relevant, creative and area specific software has been often voiced by media scholars as also by the International Commission for the Study of Communication Problems and Working Groups. The International Commission had warned that the under-development of software was a critical issue which could impede the development process otherwise envisaged by television. The Commission was of the opinion that "genuine and effective (national) independence cannot exist without the support of communication resources. It also noted that it is not only the media but the message that is important and conditions must be created to carry the cultural message."

Commenting on the expansion plans of the colour television network, Gupta (1983) pointed out that the announcement did not reflect any urgency on the part of the government about the software programming of television. Whether the government had drawn new policy perspectives as to the use of TV for national development programmes such as vocational guidance, agricultural development, educational television, family welfare and health education, was not announced. Also no reference was made to feedback, research on TV programming, etc. which brings us back to our principal dilemma; would Indian TV continue to project the Bombay film world, as also, would it continue to be the public relations outfit of the government of the day or can it be forged into a powerful instrument for national development and social change.

Elaborating on the theme of generating relevant software suited to the country, Joshi in his Sardar Patel Memorial Lectures, 1985 on 'Communication and Nation Building : Perspective and Policy, observed :

> Relevant software suited to the country can be generated with joint efforts of scientists and media men to introduce the people to the world view of the scientific age and to its fruits which help in solving the age-old and new problems of human life. Equally important is to draw upon the rich software on scientific education from developed countries and to adapt it to the country's needs.

> Collaboration in software planning with developing countries and exchange of software with them is also very urgent. Software for children is a high priority relating to science as well as culture. Further, workers and peasants organisations and activists have yet to become communication conscious using modern technology for the task of political and social education in terms of building a world-view.

In his presentation on, Communication Policy Research Agenda Workshop, at the East-West Centre, Honolulu in January 1982, N. L. Chawla observed : Communication research should not be for research sake. It should be research for 'what', to help us how to plan software. Thus, the basic components in software planning are — communication policy with clear objectives, need based, imaginative and localised programmes in addition to programmes with broader perspective, well trained communicators and well trained researchers.

Writing on the Software Dilemma, Gopal Sakesana, observed in the *Hindustan Times*, 29 August 1993:

> All the networks (including DD) would do well not to ignore the fact that television in India is quite different from what the medium stands for in the developed, westernised world. The economy social and cultural moorings and, above all, the very attitude towards life are quite different from the people of India. True, the concept of entertainment keeps on changing in every society. But while redefining it, entertainment should not divorce itself altogether from information and education, the other two universally recognised role of television.

Development and Electronic Media Policy

The objectives of television broadcasting include :

> To provide essential information and knowledge in order to stimulate greater agricultural production, to promote and help preserve environmental and ecological balance, to disseminate message of family planning as a measure of population control and family welfare, to promote national integration, to act as a catalyst for social change, etc.

Ever since the process of planned development was ushered in the country, with the launching of the First Five Year Plan in 1951, the role of communication in support of development was recognised. The Fourth

Plan document stated :

> In the spread of information facilities, the imbalance in favour of urban concentrations and prosperous areas continues. There is need for deliberate attempt to inform the people in the rural areas and particularly those in backward regions, about the specific schemes in agriculture, forestry, road construction, marketing, the supply of credit and other inputs so that the benefits of these programmes are more widely spread.

From the Sixth Five Year Plan onwards, funds allocation for electronic media, and particularly for television progressively increased. The Sixth Plan period (1980-85) saw massive expansion of Indian television. The objectives of the Seventh Five Year Plan were :

(a) National and emotional integration of various regions of the country,
(b) Utilization of the medium as a means of development and social uplift, and
(c) Dissemination of information and entertainment.

The Plan envisaged the objective of TV reaching the remotest part of the country through a "three-tier service", Primary service, National service and Local service.

Since Development, as a subject, has been discussed in greater detail in the Nation Building chapter, here it would suffice to say: Measured against the above stated objectives, Indian television has come no where near achieving these goals. Instead of working as a change agent, TV has ushered in a phase of consumerism that flaunt a highly westernised life style. Doordarshan's record in popularising development programmes on agriculture, health, consumer protection, distance education has hardly been a success. A sharper thrust, with the greater and direct involvement and participation of the target group, in the language and milieu familiar to viewers would go a long way in popularising these programmes.

Widening Gap between the Information Rich and the Information Poor

The widening gap between the information rich and the information poor. Of late, these important policy issues have invited urgent attention at several international and national fora. Concern has been expressed that television programmes have been relaying programmes with explicit over tones which have distinct and sexual violence connotations. The emerging information society which India is rapidly heading towards has the foreboding of accentuating the already yawning gap between the economically rich and economically poor. To the present situation is being added an other dimension–the yawning gap between the information rich and the information poor–the one section of the society having access to print and electronic media, as also telecommunication and other communication technology, and the other, deprived of access to these media and information technologies because of lack of economic and literacy opportunities. Both these issues have been discussed in depth in relevant chapters.

Media Impact and Regulatory Mechanisms

The phenomenal growth and the overpowering influence that electronic media has come to wield in the contemporary society has given rise to persistent debate and concern about its impact, as also envisaging the regulatory mechanism effective enough to rein in some of the adverse effects.

In the recent past the media has come under close scrutiny of the organisations, individuals and institutions, in the Parliament and through citizens groups such as parent–teacher's associations, etc. The societal issues and trends that media was considered responsible for encouraging have been many–violence, vulgarity and voyeurism, cheque book journalism, surrogate advertising, cultural alienation–are some of the issues on which attention was focussed in different occasions and in different fora.

Kitsch and the Thrill Syndrome

One of the first stirrings –rather alarm bells–on the adverse impact of cable television on young students were heard when the *Times of India* in its front page lead story with a six-column headline highlighted the search for "antidote" to counter the deleterious effect of satellite television.

Disturbed that the students in Delhi's elite schools were not keeping up with their studies and general knowledge, a teacher decided to take a close look at the reading habits of her students. She found that they have been spending upto four hours each day watching programmes which provided them entertainment, rather than education or general knowledge; television provided them with thrill. The thrill syndrome has resulted in behavioural abnormalities, reading and writing much less and generally suffering from under exposure to print. The Forum of Public Schools representing 60-odd institutions, which met to discuss how violence and promiscuity on the screen are affecting student behaviour, found out that the above trend is already causing passivity among children, leading to physical and mental retardation. As a consequence several parents decided to get the cable disconnected. The kitsch, cheapness and trivilising all the time, even normal and straight forward programmes are distorted in order to make these acceptable to the low brow, has given rise to all round and pervasive concern.

MAG Study on Obscenity and Violence

A study conducted by the Media Advocacy Group in May 1994 clearly established that parents were concerned, even apprehensive, about the impact which excessive vulgarity and violence was likely to have on their children. The programmes that the Doordarshan was telecasting were not in consonance with the ethos and values of the society. Since the study, sponsored by the Friedrich Ebert Stiftung, brings forth useful findings, it would be in order to go in some detail. The objective of the Study to create a climate for public dialogue and discussion, in the wake of an open sky policy, on obscenity and violence on the small screen; and to ensure that interests and opinions of different social groups is taken account of while framing strategies with regard to electronic media. The important findings of the Study, on Obscenity Level, are :

Spontaneously and across most segments viewers are angry and disgusted at the rising obscenity levels of films and programmes on TV. What was clear in group after group, across sex and income segments is that when sexually explicit scenes are shown on TV or there is a song with sexual innuendo there is a strong feeling of embarrassment when watching with children, sisters, brothers, parents in the home. Film songs are the worst offenders as compared with any other programme appearing on TV. There is a greater problem with the audio of film songs as compared to visuals. The songs are, however, linked because of their catchy tunes.

Since these songs and scenes are mixed up with what viewers referred to as "clean" programmes, it is very difficult to skip them. For instance, when only two or three songs from the Top Ten music programmes are vulgar, or a few minutes of a serial depict kissing or an act of intimacy, it is difficult to switch off the set while the programme is on. Programmes and films are undifferentiated to such an extent that the viewer ends up watching whatever is projected. Since the elements of sex, violence, comedy, etc. are all interwined it is difficult to reject the components they do not like.

Among young women (college going) there is a strong perception that such songs lead to eve teasing and harassment. "Comments such as 'Oye Oye, are you sexy?' make it impossible for us to walk on the streets. Men believe that all girls are like those portrayed on screen". Many of the respondents from low income groups bought television sets when *Ramayan* and *Mahabharata* were being shown. One of them said : "When we purchased these sets we did not know that such (obscene) films will be shown". It is felt that sexually explicit and kissing scenes are natural to western films and culture, "but it's not a part of our culture. It is being imposed on us."

On Violence Level, the Study observed : There is resentment of the fact that violence is being presented as entertainment. The film producers evolve new ways of showing violence, getting progressively more gruesome and sickening. Improvement in technology is being used to make the violent scenes more graphic.

Viewers believe that very often the violence depicted on screen is unnecessary. These scenes should be limited and have strong justification, such as a criminal or a wrongdoer who must be punished.

There is the perception that films are showing only the worst aspects of society, magnifying its ills and making one feel that no place is safe. "We are afraid to go out or send our daughters out," one viewer stated. Films pick up incidents from society and distort them. Viewers, across income groups, have a serious problem with the picturisation of rape scenes—it is believed that this, more than any other act of violence, corrupts the minds of children and youth.

Though there may be an excitement in watching violent scenes, and it is a form of entertainment, it is important to control the kind of violence depicted, because of the adverse effects. There is too much violence in films today because the profit motive is all important and art and culture are taking a back seat. It is felt that film-makers are making films according to the dictates of the box-office.

Regarding the impact of television on children, the Study observed : Across all income and sex groups viewers have a problem with unrestricted viewing by children. This is coupled with a helplessness felt by most to control the TV viewing by children. This is a common concern to all groups.

It is felt that TV has become almost like a member of the family and it should display the necessary responsibility, specially with respect to children. The middle and upper income segments feel that viewing of excessive violence is extremely harmful. The '*masala*' films are changing the value system of the present and future generations.

The MAG made several useful suggestions and recommendations. Some of the important recommendations are :

TV is a family medium. Programming should be sensitive to the viewers' needs. The MAG study reveals that mechanism need to be developed to ensure viewer feedback, not only on preferences, but also on expectations, reservations and objections.

Any effort to commercialise the medium at the cost of societal obligations should be avoided, particularly during prime time. Components of film based and other programmes which are obscene, derogatory to women, corrupting children and youth, or encouraging violence should not be broadcast.

Several participants in this study feel strongly that there should be segmentation of programmes. Titillating film songs should not be featured at prime time but only late at night.

If indiscriminate viewing by children has to be addressed, then media authorities need to assume equal responsibility, with parents. They will have to create the conditions that enable parents to exercise some degree of control. There should be an exclusive time slot for adult programmes.

Long term behavioural and scientific studies and audience research should be undertaken to gauge the impact of screen images and messages, on different sections of society and in particular on children and youth.

A suggestion to monitor the programmes by an independent body is significant. It is felt that censorship is not the answer, but since all the major producers and owners of satellite channels have a presence here a self-regulatory body might work.

The Special Report on Teen Spirit, referring to a landmark study of 400 American teenagers by Dr. L. Rowell Huesman and Leonard Eron of University of Illinois concludes that "heavy exposure to televised violence is one of the causes of aggressive behaviour, crime and violence in society. TV violence affects youngsters of all ages of both genders, at all socio-economic levels and all levels of intelligence.

Rising concern about juvenile delinquency, crime and general unrest and its relationship with television led to investigations by several committees and Media Task Force set up by the US Administration.

The Cultural Indicators Research Project developed a concept of television violence which concluded : For most groups of viewers, television's mean and dangerous world tends to cultivate a relative sense of fear, victimization, mistrust, insecurity and dependence, and despite its supposedly 'entertaining' nature of alienation and gloom.

The lines of research that provide some answer to the broader question of media violence and the impact it might create to different patterns of thinking and action, emerged from large scale projects of 1970 and 1980. They suggest that the violence terror scenario may have several consequences which include the cultivation of aggressive tendencies, the accommodation to violence, the depersonalization and isolation of offenders, the sporadic triggering of violent acts, and the levels of vulnerability and dependence felt by different groups living with the images of a mean and dangerous world.

Women and Cable Viewing

As a part of an international study initiated by UNESCO, to study the impact of new communication technologies on women as users and producers of the means of communication, Lalita Eashwer examined the impact of cable television on women in terms of activities, time management and interactions with family members. Some of the findings of the Study are :

Cable TV, in effect, increases considerably the isolation of women by restricting their interactions with the husband, children, other members of the family, friends and neighbours. This happens both due to their own involvement with the TV, as well as the involvement of the other members of the family, in watching the cable TV and regular TV programmes.

The second major effect of cable TV that emerges is that it restricts the exposure of the house wife to the other media including regular TV, press, radio, books, etc. As against the concentration of cable TV on movies, the other media clearly encompass a much larger horizon.

The third component of the impact of cable TV has to be seen in terms of the effect of seeing two feature films a day over an extended period. Indian feature films have always been seen as a means of escape or a form of fantasy. These feature films are the worst offenders in perpetuating violence inflicted on women and portraying a distorted and derogatory stereotype of women.

It is very important to understand what impact on overdose of this kind of fare will be on women.

The impact of cable TV could be even worse than the cinema in the original context. Exposure to feature films has, hitherto, been very selective where the women would exercise a conscious choice before going to see a movie. However, in the case of cable TV because it is there, because she is free and because two movies are screened each day, she is exposed to all kinds of feature films.

Thus, the implications of cable TV on the women are a lot more central than delays in household work or cooking and the related tensions. Cable TV has the potential for distancing women from the real world by restricting their interactions with others, restricting their horizons and bombarding them with distorted images.

Towards a Comprehensive Legal Framework

The first serious effort to legislate a comprehensive Broadcast Law was the Draft Akash Bharti Bill, 1978, proposed by the Working Group on Autonomy for Akashvani and Doordarshan. The Draft Bill intended to be an aid to legislation, provided for a simple statute establishing the National Broadcast Trust, and setting out its objectives, scope, powers and basic structure. It was, at that point of time, hoped that the Akash Bharti Act establishing the National Broadcast Trust would come into force from 1 January 1979 and Akashvani and Doordarshan will cease to be the "attached offices" of the Ministry of Information and Broadcasting.

Apart from the brief mention about the Draft Bill above, it is interesting to refer to the moving faith expressed by the Working Group in the concluding paragraph of its report :

> The conferring of "full autonomy" on a sensitive organ of information, public opinion and cultural expression is a unique act of self abnegation on the part of a government and there is no doubt that the "transfer of power" to a national broadcast trust will be complex and delicate process.

It is by now well known as to how the first effort undertaken to legislate for an autonomous broadcasting organization could not make headway due to political exigencies and lack of commitment on the part of political leadership.

It was not for another twelve years, that the Parliament in 1990, enacted the Prasar Bharati (Broadcasting Corporation of India) Act, 1990. The Act provided for the establishment of a Broadcasting Corporation of India. A unique feature of the Act was that it enlarged the definition of broadcasting, Section 2(c) as under :

> Broadcasting means the dissemination of any form of communication like signs, signals, writing, pictures, images and sounds of all kinds by transmission of electromagnetic waves through space or through cables intended to be received by the general public either directly or indirectly through the medium of relay stations and all its grammatical variations and cognate expressions shall be construed accordingly.

It is more comprehensive because it takes care of the transmission of electromagnetic waves through space or through cables. The Prasar Bharti Act aimed at creating a Broadcasting Corporation for India and the parameters within which this corporation was supposed to function. The Act provided a direction and pointer which should govern our broadcasting policies. Under Section 12(2) it was stated that the Broadcasting Corporation envisaged under the Act would be functioning and be guided by objectives such as : upholding the unity and integrity of the country and the values enshrined in the Constitution, safeguarding the citizen's rights to be informed freely, paying special attention to the fields of education, literacy, agriculture, environment, etc. providing adequate coverage to the diverse cultures, informing and stimulating the national consciousness in regard to the status and problems of women, promoting social justice, safeguarding the rights of the working classes, serving the rural and weaker sections, providing suitable programmes keeping in view the special needs of minorities and the tribal communities, taking special steps to protect the interests of children, the blind, the aged and the handicapped, and other vulnerable sections of the people, promoting national integration, providing comprehensive broadcast coverage through the choice of appropriate technology, promoting research and development activities in order to ensure that radio and television broadcasting technology are constantly updated, expanding broadcasting facilities by establishing additional channels of transmission at various levels, etc.

The Act, in terms of Section 14(1) also provided for the establishment of the Broadcasting Council, to receive and consider complaints :

From any person or group of persons alleging that a certain programme or broadcast or the functioning of the Corporation in specific cases or in general is not in accordance with the objectives for which the Corporation is established and to advise the Corporation in the discharge of its functions in accordance with the objectives set out in section 12.

According to Section I(3) of the Act, "It shall come into force on such date as the Central Government, may, by notification appoint." That notification, the Central Government has not issued for other last five years thus negating all efforts and the purpose for which the Act was passed by the Parliament.

Supreme Court Judgement

—Public Rules the Air Waves
—Freedom, One Step Closer
—Freeing the Electronic Media from Shackles

This is how the Supreme Court of India ruling delivered on 9 February 1995 on air waves was widely hailed. Since the landmark judgement of the Supreme Court, holding that air waves and frequencies were public property and asking the Central Government to establish an independent, autonomous, public authority to regulate their use; lays down important guidelines for Broadcast Law, and also enlarges the scope of Section 19 (1) of the Indian constitution, a detailed discussion of the judgement would be in order. The judgement, interalia, refers to : Freedom of Speech and Expression — includes right to acquire and disseminate information, right to communicate through any media; print, electronic or audiovisual; greater impact of TV on society — cannot afford basis for additional restrictions over and above those permissible under Article 19(2).

While resolving the litigation between the CAB and Doordarshan over uplinking of self generated signals to a foreign satellite for viewers abroad, the Court in its trend setting verdict delivered by a three-judge bench headed by Mr. Justice P. B. Sawant said that it was the fundamental right of the telecaster to "educate" the viewers' of the game, to watch the telecast was the viewers' sacred right to be entertained. An organiser like the CAB or the BCCI, could not be placed in the same scale as the business organizations .vanting to make a large profit by telecasting the series.

One of the issues discussed in these judgements is the content of the freedom of speech and expression guaranteed by Article 19(1) (a) of the Constitution. There is unanimity that the right to receive and impart information is implicit in free speech and that cricket, like any other sports event, provides entertainment which is a facet of free speech. Both judgements emphasize that it is the right of the viewers and listeners which is paramount from the stand point of Article 19(1)(a).

There is a difference of opinion over whether the right of access to air waves/frequencies can be claimed as a fundamental right by an Indian citizen. According to Justices Sawant and Mohan : The freedom of speech includes the right to disseminate information to as wide a section of the population as is possible, and therefore, the access which enables the right to be so exercised is also an integral part of the said right. The wider range of circulation of information or its greater impact cannot restrict the content of the right nor can it justify its denial. The virtues of the electronic media cannot become its enemies.

This right can be restricted but only on the grounds mentioned in Article 19(2) of the Constitution, namely, the sovereignty and integrity of India, the security of the state, friendly relations with foreign states, public order, decency or morality, contempt of court, defamation or incitement to an offence.

However, because the air waves are public property and are limited, there is an inbuilt limitation imposed by the nature of the public property involved in the use of the electronic media. Consequently, they have to be used in the best interest of the society and this can be done either by a central authority establishing its own broadcasting network or regulating the grant of licenses to other agencies including the private agencies.

The judgement unanimously lays down that, "monopoly over broadcasting whether by government or by anybody else, is inconsistent with the free speech, right of the citizens." It is rightly emphasized by Justice Reddy that, "state control really means governmental control, which, in turn, means control of the political party or parties in power for the time being. Such control is bound to colour the views, information and opinions conveyed by the media". The unanimous conclusion is that "the broadcasting media should be under the control of the public as distinct from government..... It should be operated by a public statutory corporation or corporations, as the case may be, whose constitution and composition must be such as to ensure its/their impartiality in political, economic and social matters and on all other public issues. It/they must be required by law to present news, views and opinions in a balanced way ensuring pluralism and diversity of opinions and views. It/they must provide equal access to all the citizens and groups to avail of the medium."

> Suggesting changes in the Indian Telegraph Act, 1885, which at present governs the electronic media in the country, Mr. Justice Reddy said that the Act was intended for an altogether different purpose when it was enacted. This is the result of the law in this country not keeping pace with the technological advances in the field of information and communications. Therefore, Mr. Justice Reddy suggested, it was imperative that the Parliament makes a law placing the broadcasting media in the hands of a public body. "This is necessary to safeguard the interests of public and the interests of law as also to avoid uncertainty, confusion and consequent litigation".

The Supreme Court has held that the rights of viewers are paramount; that they must participate in the affairs of the country and for that to happen they must be well informed. Says the judgement : One sided information, disinformation, misinformation and non-information, all equally create an uninformed citizenry which makes democracy a farce when the medium of information is monopolised either by a partisan central authority or by private individuals or oligarchic organizations. The answer lies in setting up of a public authority "representative of all sections of society and free from control of both the government as well as influential sections of society". The court also warned against government monopoly being replaced by that of powerful private broadcasters.

The Supreme Court Judgement has opened up exciting possibilities. Private sports casters would be allowed to buy rights from sports organizations and beam events alive, other broadcasters would have opportunity to present live news and current affairs programmes. It is felt that the judgement will eventually pave the way for the live telecast from India of programmes relating to entertainment and sports, as long as frequencies are available and Article 19(2) of the Indian Constitution is not violated.

Commenting on the judgement Amit Agarwal says :

> If the judgement is implemented in letter and spirit, it could lead to a new era in private broadcasting. It should be possible for political parties to buy time on private channels and telecast live speeches by their leaders. Similarly, Indian broadcasters will now have the right to telecast live entertainment and sports programmes, even if they are guided by commercial considerations (*India Today*, March 15, 1995).

Notwithstanding the assurances of the government to set up new public authority fairly quickly (Bhasker Ghose, *Ibid.*), frankly there is no great hope of Doordarshan getting its autonomy. In a seminar held at Bangalore in early September, Mr. Ghose stated that a comprehensive Broadcasting Act will regulate satellite channels and allow private satellite channels to uplink from within the country; however, there is no reference to the autonomy being granted to Doordarshan, which will continue to be a major player in the context of TV programming in India.

The Cable Television Network Act, 1994 was enacted with the three objectives in view. Cable operators are now legal and have three years period at their disposal to upgrade their systems to specifications. The ordinance also makes it mandatory for cable operators to adhere to the prescribed programme and advertisement code. Whereas, it is yet to be seen as to how effective implementation of the Bill would be particularly with reference to applicability of codes and inspection by officers of the Central Government; the legislation is, as one media commentator put it; "like a speed breaker at the entrance to an information super high way".

However, with the entry of big players in the cable TV industry, and poor infrastructure, the industry presents a chaotic market. Licenses and permissions are not forthcoming in spite of the Cable TV Act, which says that each state government will have to evolve a policy on how the cables are to be laid.

Quality of TV Programmes

It was indeed startling to know that the Chairman of the National Human Rights Commission, Mr. Justice Ranganath Misra sought the support of the United Nations in dealing with violence on television. Speaking recently on the activities of the Commission at the Centre for Strategic and International Studies in Washington, Mr. Mishra said that he had written to the US Secretary General, Mr. Boutros Ghali on the subject of violence on television which militated against the concept of human rights. He said his commission was trying to stop projection of violence on the Indian television, but foreign television shows, now available in the country, depicted violence in a big way.

In a seminar organised by the Asian Mass Communication, Research and Information Centre, at Kuala Lumpur in August 1995 on Asian Values in Journalism, the Information Minister of Malaysia in his inaugural address, gave two examples of trivialising our cultural traditions by foreign TV networks and both the examples were from India : The abusive expression used against Mahatma Gandhi in the STAR television programme hosted by Nikki Bedi; and the newsclip of cows straddling the Bombay streets shown on the occasion of the launching of CNN Doordarshan agreement. In both cases, sensitivities of the Indian viewers were deeply hurt. These instances were not the only one which have evoked concern and unhappiness about the values that the Indian television tends to foster. Media analysts and commentators have pointed to the country lacking a TV policy which would promote relevant, good quality programmes while discouraging competitive mindlessness and vulgarity

In this free-for-all scenario, there has been a steady deterioration in the quality of most programmes. The President of the Cable Operators Association, Roopa Sharma says, she receives more and more complaints about explicitly sexual sequences included in programmes for universal distribution. Most entertainment channels are slaves to glitzy western consumerism and sex and violence themes.

India is increasingly becoming the playing field of the world's biggest media players for their share of our unregulated 15 million homes cable TV market run by 60,000 operators. This market is bigger than that of any country in Europe barring Russia and Germany.

The Ministry of Information and Broadcasting and Doordarshan, rather than encouraging and producing good quality programmes, claim to break new ground by doubling its viewer ratings and income by retransmitting filmy trash.

Television in India has failed to offer any perspective on information, education or entertainments. Information is reduced to entertainment, and the latter to triviality. The mandate of television is not to make super-profits, but to make good programmes.

In one of his leading articles, Parful Bidwai says :

> What we need is a comprehensive policy to promote high quality, independent, credible and competent television, which is at least as good as our press. This can only be done if DD is replaced by an independent authority and restructured so that professionals replace bureaucrats and sycophants. Its newsroom must be placed under the control of a neutral body of well trained journalists. It should be mandated to promote quality entertainment."

Marginalisation of Radio

The Working Group on Autonomy for Akashvani and Doordarshan had recommended :

> 20.2 : The Working Group is of the view that while television is a powerful and effective medium, there is no doubt that India should give first priority to the development and densification of radio for at least the next 10 to 15 years. Radio is far cheaper and the availability of cheap transistors has made it ubiquitous. The country, however, has a long way to go before it can even begin to think that it has substantially exploited the potential of radio.

Had the above recommendation been implemented, media situation in the country would have been more vibrant, meaningful and relevant to the development needs of the people in the country.

The following excerpt from 'Communication Policies in India' is as relevant today as it was thirty years ago :

> In a country of India's size with four-fifths of the people living in villages, radio is the only means of mass communication. It can reach the remotest areas and involve the people in the processes of growth and change. The role of radio has rightly been pointed out

> in a paper submitted to a meeting on developing mass media in Asia, convened in 1960 by UNESCO at Bangkok :
>
> In Asia and its periphery, the power of radio is especially great because of the unquestioning receptivity of the illiterate masses. To them the spoken word, coming instantaneously on the air, has an oracular authority. News heard by radio is repeated by word of mouth in the Bazaars and village gatherings till the circulation gained defies all calculations based on the percentage of owners of sets.

The rapid expansion in the FM radio broadcasting in recent years has brought radio back in the communication media priorities. Radio is no longer considered as an 'ancient relic' or an attic treasure — relegated to a historical past, preserved for sentimental value rather than for its functional use. The decision of the government to allot time slots to private producers on FM channels of AIR in the four metropolitan cities of Bombay, Calcutta, Delhi and Madras; putting out live phone-in-Programmes; the Radio Network — the Calcutta based radio channel with Mark Tully as the guiding spirit, are some of the bold and innovative initiatives which are bound to bring back radio to the centre stage of media world, bustling and booming with excitement and expansion.

Radio for Development

As a tool for development, radio continues to remain unsurpassed because of its easy accessibility, cost effectiveness and localness of the medium. Since television is being driven, more and more by advertising and market forces, the objective of using it as a tool for development has long been relegated to side ways. In fact a stage has reached where even the pretence of the use of television for development is not even being maintained. On television, it is soaps, films and film songs, with news bulletins related to mostly government functionaries in government related and sponsored functions; with some programmes on science and environment thrown in. In such a situation it would be once again important to underline the importance of radio for development.

The Radio Farm Forum Project, organised in, Poona, ushered in "rural development broadcasting" on a large scale. The Farm and Home programmes presently in 92 AIR stations, besides Local Radio Stations constitute hard core development programmes for a large segment of rural population. With the concept of Local Radio Stations expanding rapidly, area specific development programmes catering to the needs and aspirations of local population, would further enhance radio's contribution to rural development programmes in the country.

Commenting on the role of radio for development, Misra has very aptly pointed : Every medium of communication has cultural identity and away from this, it tends to lose its effectiveness. Over the years radio has created for itself an image of being an important source of education and development. This has been possible because of its history of putting out programmes related to social and civic problems, agricultural programmes, health, family planning and nutrition related programmes, and on formal and non-formal education broadcasts. The other tele-electronic medium, that is television, on the other hand has evolved for itself an image of being essentially an entertainment medium and even as an extended arm of the film industry.

The cost effectiveness here denotes the capacity of the medium in reaching messages to a large population in comparatively cheaper terms as compared to other media. This applies to cost both at the transmitting and the receiving ends. Judged by this criterion, radio emerges as the most cost-effective medium. Estimatedly a one hour colour television transmission may cost ten times more than the radio transmission of the same duration. At the receiving end, a cheap transistor set can cost as little as 40 rupees with practically negligible running costs. No other medium can compare with it. In terms of recording the programmes, again the radio equipments do not require costly paraphernalia as in the case of television or films.

He also says : AIR also has a tradition of focussing on specific target groups through its special audience broadcasts such as women's programmes, farm and home broadcasts, youth programmes, industrial workers programmes, broadcasts for tribal populations, etc. These are composite programmes and include music, talks, request programmes, skits, etc. An important feature of these programmes is that they focus on the specific problems of the target groups and provide relevant information as well as possible solutions for them. The special audience broadcasts have considerably high listenership among the target audience.

It is, therefore, essential to reiterate that the broadcasting policy be given a critical look keeping in view the primacy that radio would continue enjoy in terms of accessibility, cost-effectiveness and reach over television for development and educational purposes, whatever might be the entertainment value of the television programmes. In this context, Mehra Masani has rightly pointed out : Broadcasting cannot play any significant role in our lives unless there is clear thinking on a number of issues.

Indian public opinion has to be mobilised to play a much more active part in deciding what kind of broadcasting it wants and what its role should be, particularly in supporting the great national tasks. The present confusion of aims and contradictory policies, undisputed and unchallenged by the public, save in the most perfunctory manner, are retarding the growth of the broadcasting.

Communication system decisions made today will affect what will be available fifty years hence. It is, therefore, imperative that everywhere the broadcasting policy and broadcasting laws are geared to serve the society for the greatest good of the largest number of people. That should be the vision and the philosophy permeating our broadcast media.

REFERENCES

Akash Bharati : National Broadcast Trust, Vol. I. (1978). Report of the Working Group on Autonomy for Akashvani and Doordarshan. New Delhi : Ministry of Information and Broadcasting, p. 108.

Ammu Joseph and Sharma, Kalpna (eds.) (1994). *Whose News ? The Media and Women's Issues.* Sage Publications Ltd., New Delhi.

An Indian Personality for TV, Vol. I (1985). Report of the Working Group on Software for Doordarshan. New Delhi : Publications Division. pp. 116-121.

Acharya, R. N. (1987). *Television in India.* New Delhi : Manas Publications. p. 55.

Chawla, N. L. (1982). Communication Policy in India—Software Production and Distribution. *Communicator,* **XVII** (1) : 2-6, 10.

Eighth Five Year Plan (1992-97). Objectives. New Delhi : Planning Commission.

Gupta, V. S. (1995). *Third Revolution in Indian Perspective — Contemporary Issues and Themes in Communication.* Concept Publishing Company, New Delhi.

Joshi, P. C. (1986). Communication and Nation Building : Perspective and Policy, Sardar Patel Memorial Lectures (1985). New Delhi : Publications Division.

Lee, John A. R. (1976). Towards Realistic Communication Policies : Recent trends and ideas compiled and analysed. UNESCO.

Menon, Narayana (1976). *The Communication Revolution.* New Delhi : National Book Trust. p. 86.

Sawant, B. P., S. Mohan and Reddy, B. P. Jeevan (1995). Supreme Court Judgement in Civil Appeals No. 1429-30 : Secretary, Ministry of Information and Broadcasting *vs* Cricket Association of India.

Singhal, Arvind and Rogers, Everett, M. (1989). *India's Information Revolution.* New Delhi : Sage.

Srivastava, U. K. (1987). National Cost of Television in India in the Year 2000 : Socio-Economic and Political Issues. *Media Asia,* **14** (3) : 136-144.

UNESCO (1980). *Many Voices, One World.* The International Commission for the Study of Communication Problems.

7

MEDIA CODES, GUIDELINES AND REGULATORY MEASURES

The media—both print as well as electronic in the country severely need effective watchdog mechanism, media monitors and regulatory measures so as to make media subserve the larger social purpose rather than that of the government of the day, which more often than not, use the media apparatus, particularly the electronic media for partisan ends and party propaganda. The urgent necessity of public accountability of media through national bodies constituted of professionals, public persons, activist groups and voluntary organisations has been felt for a long time, more so in the recent past. These are essential to bring about a semblence of order in an otherwise expanding and chaotic media scenario.

Some of these watchdog mechanisms and regulatory measures are already in place—Press Council of India being the most well known; Broadcasting Council envisaged in the Prasar Bharti Bill has not been constituted. Several media organisations, advertising industry and professional bodies have their codes and guidelines for regulating the profession and setting suitable standards.

Press Council of India

In a paper by the Press Council Chairman, Justice A. N. Grover, published in *Vidura* in February 1980 (reprinted, January-February 1991), it has been pointed out that the Press Council can act not only as the Ombudsman for the press but can also perform the functions of a watchdog for the preservation of its freedom and maintenance of its responsibility and accountability to the people, but that will require an all effort from all directions, the press itself, the government and the people to attain these goals. Elaborating its working, role and importance, Justice Grover stated: The Council is a highly representative and strong body with powers even to make observations respecting the conduct of any authority including the government in addition to having the power to warn, admonish or censure the newspaper, the news agency, the editor or the journalist who has offended against the standards of journalistic ethics or public taste. The procedure that has to be followed is of a quasi-judicial nature and the Council has been vested with the powers of a civil court with regard to summoning of witnesses, discovery and inspection of documents, receiving evidence, requisitioning public records, etc.

The matters that have come before the Press Council are not confined only to the domain of politics. They relate to laws of libel, obscenity and contempt and cover criminal trials as well. Resort to a court of law is not only expensive but also is sometimes very tedious and cumbersome. Thus, cases which involve invasion of privacy have been brought before the Press Council.

The tasks that the Indian Press Council has been called upon to perform by the statutory provisions are manifold. It has not only to help newspapers and news agencies to maintain independence, but also to build up principles for the maintenance of high standards of journalistic profession with a stress on public taste, and fostering of a due sense of rights and responsibilities of citizenship.

However, it has also been observed that if a newspaper chooses to be recalcitrant, the Council is helpless. There have been repeated suggestions that the Press Council Act be amended to empower it to recommend to the central or state governments or other public bodies, etc. stoppage of issue of advertisements, curtailment in the matter of allocation of newsprint or suspension of concessional rates of postage, for a specified period, in the case of newspapers which are censured thrice. In the case of journalists and editors, who are held by the Council thrice to have violated the accepted principles of journalistic ethics, the Council desires to have the power to deny facilities of accredition for a specified period.

There has been some debate on whether or not the powers conferred on the Press Council are adequate to enable it to function as a watchdog of the press. Critics of the Council argue that it lacks teeth to punish or deter sufficiently an erring newspaper or journalist as any censure or admonition administered by it can be — and often is — brazenly ignored by the offending newspaper or journalist, leaving the complainant far from satisfied. The government has, however, thought it fit to let the Council remain a persuasive and reformative body rather than one with punitive powers.

Ombudsman

In the context of media monitors, the institution of Ombudsman has come in for reference. The word Ombudsman has its origin in Sweden and Denmark. The word Ombudsman would mean grievance man, an official appointed to investigate the complaints against the administration. The appointment of an Ombudsman by the *Times of India* a few years back was widely commended.

The *Times of India* had clearly laid down the duties and responsibilities of the Ombudsman and the manner of submitting complaints to him. He will not directly receive complaints but will deal only with those that are specifically referred to him by the editor. All complaints are to be addressed to the editor, in the first place, who will examine them and take the necessary corrective action including referring the complaints to the Ombudsman. It lays down that while it agrees to abide by the verdict of the Ombudsman in every case (or else, what would be the point in having one?), "even though it might not necessarily agree with it", the complainant shall also give a similar prior undertaking that he will accept the verdict of the Ombudsman and abide by it.

However, the working and the effectiveness of the Ombudsman in the *Times of India* remains a question mark.

The *Asian Mass Communication Bulletin* (20 : 2) reported the appointment of Ombudsman by a leading Japanese daily. In Japan, *Asahi Shimbun*, one of the country's largest newspapers, has established an Advisory Press Council to act as its Ombudsman and two other organizations — the Public Affairs Office and Monitoring Editors.

The Council is an advisory body responsible to the company's President. It is made up of five members comprising lawyers and distinguished ex-journalists.

Its functions include submitting findings on the contents of newspapers and magazines and reporting on readers' complaints to the President. It has also been given the right to ask various departments in the head office to study and report on questionable matters.

The main duties of the Monitoring Editors are to ensure news stories are factually sound and fair, and that the appropriate amount of space is allotted to articles.

The formation of these bodies by a newspaper is something new for the Japanese press but with *Asahi* taking the lead and determined to ensure that the system benefits its publications, other papers are expected to follow suit if only to please their readers.

Broadcasting Council

The establishment of Broadcasting Council, which was envisaged by the Prasar Bharati Act 1990, would have rightly served as the Ombudsman for the electronic media. The Act under section 15 stipulated that the Broadcasting Council would receive and consider complaints from :

> 15 (i) : any person or group of persons alleging that a certain programme or broadcast or the functioning of the Corporation in specific cases or in general is not in accordance with the objectives for which the Corporation is established;
>
> 15 (ii) : any person, other than an officer or employee of the Corporation, claiming himself to have been treated unjustly or unfairly in any manner (including unwarranted invasion of privacy, misrepresentation, distortion or lack of objectivity) in connection with any programme broadcast by the Corporation.

The Varadan Committee set up by the government for the regulation of satellite and cable TV suggested that this body (Broadcasting Council of India) be entrusted with the functions in respect of licensing of cable network operators, as against the option of the government issuing licences for a new channel, as well as monitoring and quality of programmes.

Stressing the imperative urgency of establishing a watchdog mechanism, Sevanti Ninan (1994) said : Clearly some kind of watchdog body is needed to end the practice of allowing every Minister of Information and Broadcasting who comes along to treat Doordarshan as his personal *jagirdari.* Is State owned TV supposed to serve the ruling party and its minions or the people? Silly of me to ask, I should know the answer, but may I suggest we viewers attempt to change the answer to that question?

Of late there has been little talk of setting up the Broadcasting Council. But increasingly as vulgarity and misuse of air time on television increases, as public grievances against TV channels, both indigenous and foreign proliferate, public and legislative pressure needs to be built up to set up such a council so that the working of the government controlled electronic media is held properly accountable.

Instances of misuse of electronic media, violation of the guidelines governing the News Policy for Broadcasting Media, have been documented and commented upon on numerous occasions, with hardly any redressal. Instances of partisan conduct on the part of both these media have multiplied to the point where AIR and Doordarshan have almost lost their credibility. Apart from giving disproportionately large coverage to the ruling party and its members, especially to those in government, these media have also on occasion, displayed a degree of political partisanship that makes charges of gross ministerial and bureaucratic interference unanswerable.

Advertising Standards Council of India

The advertising industry has frequently come in for criticism from the public for, among other things, putting out misleading or exaggerated claims in respect of goods and services, glorifying certain habits or tendencies regarded as undesirable, and stimulating expectations amongst those who may not be able to fulfil them. This has generally led to demands for stricter legal controls which in turn have been resisted by the industry with the offer of a system of self-regulation.

One of the concrete measures adopted towards such self-regulation is a Code formulated by the ASCI, a professional body set up by the industry not so long ago. The Code prescribes a set of standards which the industry is expected to follow and is couched in fairly general terms. Complaints about breaches of the Code can be made to a Consumer Complaints Council for adjudication. This system obviously lacks the deterrent of penal sanctions that a legally enforceable regulatory measure would contain, but the industry argues that censure by their peers is a sufficient enough deterrent to advertisers in most cases. The Code came into force in 1985.

Surrogate Advertising

The practice of surrogate advertising by the liquor industry has come in for severe criticism by the advertising industry itself. In a seminar on "self-regulation or pre-censorship" held in Bombay in January 1995, the Chairman of Radeus Advertising K. Kurian said : By promoting their products through surrogate advertising certain liquor manufacturers are destroying the credibility of advertising itself. He said that such a "con job" gave "credence to the belief that advertising is the art of converting a complete lie into a half-truth".

It was, therefore, suggested that ASCI, in conjuction with other media organisations evolve common guidelines for self-regulation in advertising, with consequent penalties. The codes and guidelines, evolved by the professional bodies notwithstanding, there has been a general dissatisfaction with the implementation and working of these guidelines.

Instances of chequebook journalism, low brow fare dished by the highly commercialised government controlled electronic media have been documented elsewhere in the various chapters of this book.

Pointing out to the, Deviation between Laws and Codes as Written and Actual Practice, K. S. Venkateswaran in his book, *Mass Media Laws and Regulations in India* (1993) points out :

> Complaints have ranged from grossly disproportionate use of broadcast time to present the ruling party's viewpoint to the near total exclusion of other view points, denial of access to those representing opposing, non-conformist or minority interests, blatant distortion of news to the government's advantage and so on, complaints which are not always amenable to judicial adjudication. The absence of an independent watchdog to which the aggrieved can turn, has only served to exacerbate the consequent feeling of helplessness engendered in the community. It is a measure of the frustration felt on this score that some public spirited citizens have, as noted earlier, begun approaching the courts to challenge the state monopoly over radio and television.

REFERENCES

AMIC (1990). Ombudsman for leading Japanese daily. *Asian Mass Communication Bulletin*, **20** (2). Singapore.

Grover, A. N. (1991). Press Council in a Democratic Society. *Vidura*. Press Institute of India, New Delhi.

Kamath, M. V. (1989). Does Ombudsman make Press Council redundant. *Mid-Day*, 23 January, Bombay.

Times of India (1995). Surrogate Advertising decried by ad world, 16 January.

Venkateswaran, K. S. (1993). *Mass Media Laws and Regulations in India*. Asian Mass Communication Research and Information Centre.

8

CONCLUSION AND RECOMMENDATIONS

The formulation of a National Media Policy, at best of times, is one of the most complex tasks, and more so when the media technologies are expanding fast, and societal and political considerations are becoming more competitive. There has been a body of opinion that we would be far better off without a media policy, broad guidelines and professional codes would do. However, there are issues of national import which need to be articulated and have been discussed in the preceding chapters.

There has also been a legitimate question as to who should be entrusted with the formulation of the National Media Policy — perhaps constitution of an independent Media Commission, comprising eminent media experts, representatives of non-government and voluntary bodies working in this area, eminent public persons and professional film makers, broadcasters, print journalists and representatives from Parliament, would inspire sufficient public confidence for initiating such an exercise. Even then the task would be colossal and opinions, at times, sharply differing. It would, at the same time, be imperative that such a policy should have broad appeal and acceptance which would be possible through a consesual approach which would take into account legitimate concerns of every section of the society. Another associated issue would be : implementation of the National Media Policy. Do we have a statutory organisation like Press Council of India, or a parliamentry body representing both houses of Parliament?

These issues do not admit easy solutions. At the same time, we thought it fit, that at the time of the on-going debate in this area we would do well to focus attention on some of the proposals which help enhancing the quality of programmes for rural areas, and development and educational purposes, as also provide a platform to media advocacy and public interest groups, as have been in existence in several other countries.

Exclusive TV and Radio Channel for Increased Rural Programmes

An exclusive channel on TV and Radio for rural programmes — Rural Channel - is envisaged for enhancing the quality, frequency and priority of programmes for rural areas. These programmes could also broadcast traditional entertainment and cultural programmes so popular in villages. Development messages, through traditional cultural entertainment programmes, are received by rural audience with great interest. In the absence of such a channel, the felt needs of the rural community get lost or crowded out in the competing demands for entertainment from urban audience.

More electronic media programmes must emanate from the villages, with common issues and problems and from the farmer's fields. Television must not only produce programmes for the rural people but also of the rural people; let it present what the rural people think of themselves and what solutions do they offer for their problems. Let the television not present, as the Report of the Working Group on Software for Doordarshan, pointed out, "an urban view of rural problems or a view of the problems of urbanised villages."

Training Programmes for Rural Journalists

Training programmes for workers in rural development projects like village level workers in communication methods and those of communication practitioners in rural development would go a long way in creating the much needed mutual appreciation of both the aspects. Since, with the expansion of the print media the problems of staff training and recruitment are getting bigger every year, inhouse training should be organised by the newspapers, besides formal training in journalism schools. An appreciation course in rural problems, preferably a rural institute or an agricultural university, would go a long way in redressing this deficiency. A Consultancy Service for the rural press or for those national newspapers who want to report on rural problems would fulfil the objective in a large measure. It has also been observed that the personnel working in the rural press lack adequate training required to handle their multifaceted responsibilities. They lack not only adequate editorial ability, but also the perspective necessary to manage various aspects of a newspaper. Rural papers also lack balance— the papers coming out from government or semi-government organisations avoid giving community or political news and thereby fail to create broad interest in the reading public. Training would help the rural journalists not only to acquire the perspective of a complete newspaper, but also to evolve an ideal editorial mix.

It would be advisable to institute Journalists Fellowship Awards for persons working in the area of rural development reporting and communication. The Fellowship would enable the working mediamen, to work during the Fellowship period, on a selected project and make an indepth study of the subject. Salary for the Fellowship period and travel grant would meet the expenses. Such Fellowships have been instituted by the Ministry of Environment, Forests and Wildlife as a part of National Environment Awareness Campaign.

Extension Agency Reinforcement

Radio and TV broadcasting, essentially a part of mass media communication process, shares the characteristics and limitations of such a system. In such a system amount of feedback readily available is low, the message flow tends to be one way and can be used to increase knowledge. Interpersonal medium, on the other hand, tends to be two-way and the amount of feedback readily available is high and is best used in situations calling for attitude formation and change.

Interpersonal medium, which in the context of rural development, would include extension workers in the agriculture and community development departments of the state governments, personnel of agricultural agencies like MAFAL and agro-industries centres and extension set up of agricultural universities and research institutes, would provide necessary reinforcement and supplement media programmes. Coordination between extension agencies and rural broadcasting will make these programmes more purposive and meaningful. These agencies can, in fact, help disseminate information about media programmes including topics and subjects for discussion through numerous magazines, leaflets, folders they bring out regularly and on special occasions like farmers fairs and field days, as a part of their extension activities. They can also involve programme producers and planners in programme formulation and modify programmes to suit the requirement of the target audience.

Such institutionalised working relationship and coordination will help to serve the rural population better and contribute to the tasks of rural development which is the central objective of communication policies and programmes.

National Council for Mass Communication

One of the earliest proposals of the Committee on Broadcasting and Information Media (1964), to the implementation of which the government had actually agreed was the formation of the National Council for Mass

Communication. As envisaged, such a Council would be a well informed representative and broad based body comprising officials as well as eminent non-officials to advise on the role and performance on the mass communication media, including their coordinated growth. The Chanda Committee also visualised the Council to be autonomous body and not subordinate to the Ministry of Information and Broadcasting. It should have the professional status to advise the government on policy for all media of communication, traditional and modern, and on future developments such as satellites, cable TV and others. Representatives of the press, publishing, advertising, films, and of the union and state governments must find a place on the Council.

Masani (1976) enlarging on the concept of the National Council for Mass Communication, suggested that the Council should also ensure coordination between the media and the agencies responsible for development policies including the Planning Commission, the Ministries and departments of government. It could usefully undertake manpower planning for the media and provide for the evaluation of their performance particularly the programmes of social education. Masani's observations succinctly sum up the situation of broadcasting in the country as under :

> Broadcasting cannot play any significant role in our lives unless there is clear thinking on a number of issues. Indian public opinion has to be mobilised to play a much active part in deciding what kind of broadcasting it wants and what its role should be, particularly in supporting the great national tasks. The present confusion of aims and contradictory policies, undisputed and unchallenged by the public, save in the most perfunctory manner, are retarding the growth of broadcasting.

The National Council will go a long way in meeting the above objectives and also in educating public opinion about the imperative need of inculcating a healthy broadcasting culture in the society.

National Council for Listeners and Viewers

It is being increasingly realised that only a strong public opinion, articulated through properly constituted forum representing a broad cross section of society, like Media Advocacy Groups, Public Interest Organisations or other media watchdog mechanism could play an interventionist role in ensuring healthy and creative media programmes.

The Korean television audiences have constituted "Task-force groups" for concentrating on specific areas of broadcasting such as children programming, entertainment, news and advertising, group members are concerned about broadcasting law, objectivity and fairness of news coverage, violence in children's programmes and commercialization of sex, gender discrimination, etc. TV monitoring is being undertaken by such groups through training courses for the staff and volunteers of other interested organizations.

In Britain there is a Viewers' and Listeners' Association and Radio and TV Committee in which writers and academics are represented. Such groups can certainly play useful role in sensitising public opinion against objectionable and pernicious trends in TV programming. Whenever public opinion through an organised representative forum asserts itself the government has to take note of their perceptions.

In this context, Rao (1988) has pointed out : A monopoly should entail restraint by the monopolists as well as responsiveness to public demands and needs. Both Doordarshan and viewers must interact. It is time that people in general and viewing households in particular came together to "talk back" to TV as moderators of the system. When rail passengers and telephone subscribers can form groups to protect their collective interest all over India, why not a TV Viewers' Council of each TV Centre? It is odd that despite its ubiquitousness, TV has not generated a consumer movement of its own. As a result, the public dissatisfaction with TV can only increase. Autonomy or no automony, the need to "talk back" to TV is immense. Keeping television relevant, responsive, democratic and progressive is a matter requiring the constant vigilance of all viewers. Television should be kept from feeling it is infallible and invulnerable and so from becoming tyrannical. Public scepticism towards it is a vital ingredient in improving its quality. However, there is an imperative need to channelize public scepticism into a responsive, constructive and positive platform.

Franchise Stations

The enormous potential of utilizing franchise stations for education, teaching and training purposes has been repeatedly stressed at various fora. As Dua (1980) points out : So far very little is known in this country about the purpose and functions of such franchise stations. In western countries, especially the United States, the departments of journalism and mass communication of nearly all universities operate atleast one radio station, a television centre and a film studio. These media are exclusively run and operated by students of journalism and mass communication departments. Reporting, writing and broadcasting and also conducting the affairs of radio and television stations are part of academic instruction and training for mass communication students.

The Working Group on Autonomy for Akashvani and Doordarshan, while recommending the institution of franchise stations stated :

> We accordingly recommend that the National Broadcast Trust be authorised to grant a broadcast franchise, whether for radio or television, to approved educational institutions. Such a franchise recommendation by the National Broadcast Trust should automatically be converted into a broadcast licence by the Ministry of Communications, the specific frequencies being allocated and coordinated by the Ministry's Wireless Adviser.

We see several advantages in developing a system of franchise stations on the lines indicated. These would not only bring variety and innovation to programming but would give a powerful stimulus to educational and extension broadcasting. They would enhance participation and access and involve young people in broadcasting as well as in the development of hardware and software systems and of communication policy. These broadcast stations could be used as internal teaching aids, as for example, by the departments of medicine and engineering, education, communication and journalism, and by the physics and electronics faculties. The cultural faculties of universities would also be able to use the broadcast facility to enhance the creative talents of the student community.

The franchise stations for agricultural universities would go a long way in reinforcing the extension work of the universities, apart from teaching and training purposes which could also be fulfilled through such stations. Kheda Communication Project, run by the Space Application Centre, has successfully shown as to how such communication development programmes can be successfully executed.

The National Workshop on Akash Bharati convened by IARI (1978) while endorsing the recommendations of the Working Group said : The Workshop accepted the recommendations of the Working Group on establishing Franchise Stations in institutions like Agricultural Universities, Central Research Institutes and other institutions which have an educational, extension or cultural orientation.

There should be a continuous inflow of information on achievements of proven value in terms of research and extension communication covering problems for the benefit of the various rural people for increasing the farm production and also helping in better living. Regarding the question of the franchise stations being permitted to relay news bulletins or commercial advertisements, the Workshop recommended that the developmental news may be broadcast, in the form of Farm and Home Round-up twice a week or so. It would be worthwhile to consider implementing the above recommendations and instituting franchise stations for training and academic purposes.

EPILOGUE

All through the last year when we were working on the book, our one effort was to keep ourselves updated with the latest trends, views and publications. We were also looking for the reaffirmation, if any, of our views, and the extent to which professionals in other areas — economists, social scientists, public men and media experts thought that media could be effectively used in some of the nation building tasks, we had indicated in our book.

We have been amply rewarded for our efforts. Some of the books released and reviewed during the later part of the year have affirmed that media could indeed be harnessed for several of the tasks associated with nation building.

Controlled Press and Public Media — The Chinese Example

In *India — Economic Development and Social Opportunity*, Dreze and Sen (1995), while analysing the reasons for the frequent occurrence of famines in China, point out that the Chinese government did not wake up to the nature and magnitude of the calamity for quite a long time and the disastrous policies were not substantially revised for three years, while the famine raged on because of the *informational failure*. The informational failure, linked to controlled press, duped not only the public in suppressing information about the famine, but the government was also deluded as well. Whereas in a democratic country, no substantial famine has ever occurred, because the government which has to deal with opposition parties, face condemnation from *public media*, and to go to polls on a regular basis, cannot afford not to take prompt action to avert threatening famine.

However, the reach of public criticism can be less effective when the deprivations are less extreme or are of regular occurrence, under nourishment and economic insecurity, lack of school facilities and clean drinking water, may not receive critical attention depending upon the particular nature of politics and journalism in the regions involved.

The book strongly underlines the role of public activism in influencing government policy in promoting positive functions of the government which would include provision of basic public services such as health care, child immunization, primary education, social security, environmental protection, and rural infrastructure (p. 89). In promoting *public activism and public action*, India's democratic institutions including electoral process but also news media, the legal systems, village panchayats, etc. can provide potential basis (p. 191).

The publication, which has become almost a classic on women's movement — *A Field of One's Own, Gender and Land Rights in South Asia*, Bina Agarwal (1995) underlines the role of media in influencing public opinion for bargaining with State on gender issues. Agarwal says : The leverage that gender progressive groups in 'bargaining' with the State can have depend on a variety of factors : their ability to sway public opinion or to disrupt administrative functioning (through agitations); the political pressure they can build up in various ways, with implications for voting patterns; the attention they can get for their cause through the media; their ability to deliver programmes which State agencies are unable to deliver by themselves; the existence of pressure for gender sensitivity from international aid agencies; and so on.

In the chapter, From Sermons to Sitcoms : A History, in her book, *Through the Magic Window—Television and Change in India* (1995), Sevanti Ninan recapitulates how in the brief history of Doordarshan, Development Communication has given way to straight forward commercial survival in the era of satellite competition from abroad. In the beginning, the prevailing ideology was television for development. Thereafter, its importance diminished, never to regain supremacy again, except in rhetoric. Ninan concludes the chapter with an observation, which has found echo in the deliberations and proceedings of several seminars : Today a revitalized Doordarshan is ready to take on rival channels, *but the only thing it does not do with any marked degree of enthusiasm is fulfil its once-upon-a-time role as a catalyst for the development of the downtrodden Indian.* In this country, development communication is still waiting to happen (p. 41). Ninan also refers to the Report of the Working Group for Software for Doordarshan — A Personality for Television (1985), which had underlined the need to prevent 'the appropriation of television by the emerging forces of commercialism and consumerism'. To the disappointment and concern of discerning public, the market forces are all over the Indian media system as never before.

Apart from the contribution of the media to the nation building tasks, the present work has attempted to focus the imperative urgency to impart autonomy to the government controlled electronic media. The Central Government does not seem to be in a hurry to implement the landmark Supreme Court Judgement, pronounced in February last year. Referring to the desperate efforts of the government to retain control over radio and television, T. N. Seshan says in his book, *The Degeneration of India* (1995) : But arguably the greatest damage to media credibility in this country, has come as a result of the Central Government's control over radio and television. Now, in a ludicrous piece of manoeuvring, the government is scrambling to keep pace with world-wide changes in the media without letting go of its iron hold on Doordarshan and radio. The result is foregone : all changes will be cosmetic and insubstantial and the general standard of information and news dissemination will remain as woefully inadequate and skewed as before. If government is practical, it will realize that it cannot control the media, especially the electronic media forever, especially given the fact that any changes that will take place will be technology driven, and technological innovation always takes place faster than the deployment of any controls to throttle it. Indeed, the government would be wise to review relatively recent history.

Just as we conclude our efforts, we are convinced that given the freedom and autonomy to the electronic media, its potential can be truly exploited for the tasks of nation building, forces of commercialisation and consumerism notwithstanding. We are also convinced that given the will, right priorities and perspectives, the immense potential of media systems can certainly be harnessed for the progress and the good of the country.

We will consider our task well done and our efforts worthwhile, if it stimulates reflection about the potential and urgency of harnessing the media for the building of the Indian society. If it provokes the policy makers, scholars and readers to re-examine media issues in the context of what we have outlined in the book, we would consider our efforts amply rewarded.

REFERENCES

Agarwal, Bina (1995). *A Field of One's Own — Gender and Land Rights in South Asia.* Cambridge University Press.

Dreze, Jean and Sen, Amartya (1995). *India —Economic Development and Social Opportunity.* Oxford University Press, Delhi.

Garg, Pulin K. and Parikh, Indira J. (1995). *Crossroads of Culture — A Study in the Culture of Transience.* New Delhi : Sage.

Ninan, Sevanti (1995). *Through the Magic Window — Television and Change in India.* Penguin Books, New Delhi

The Degeneration of India (1995). T. N. Seshan with Sanjoy Hazarika, Viking, New Delhi.

Epilogue

ANNEXURES

ANNEXURE I

PRESS IN INDIA AT A GLANCE IN 1993

Number of Newspapers

Dailies	3,740
Tri/Bi-Weeklies	275
Weeklies	11,136
Fortnightlies	4,571
Monthlies	9,837
Others	4,053
Total	33,512
Miscellaneous Publications	3,162
Total on record	36,774

Circulation of Newspapers	(in thousands)
Dailies	29,258
Tri/Bi-Weeklies	230
Weeklies	21,380
Fortnightlies	5, 807
Monthlies	9, 860
Others	1, 076
Total	67, 611

ANNEXURE II

GROWING SATELLITE CHANNELS AND EXPANDING DOORDARSHAN NETWORK

Liberalisation of the airwaves has resulted in a proliferation of satellite television channels in India. Doordarshan began telecast on as many as 13 channels on Independence Day, 1994 making available at least 25 channels for the viewers to choose from. They include CNN, BBC, Star Plus, Prime Sports, V, Zee, Jain, Sun, Asianet and ATN. Some others are in the offing too.

Some analysts predict that as many as 50 channels might be broadcasting by 1995 when new satellites like APSTAR-2, Panam-Sat, Asia Sat-2 and INSAT-2C will be launched.

The enlarged Doordarshan telecast meant that for the first time, it brought individual *kendras* on the satellite networks, with each channel being uplinked from individual *kendras* instead of from Delhi.

Primary channel (DD1) continues to remain the only fully terrestrial channel all over the country. DD2 is being telecast terrestrially from 15 *kendras* that include the four metros of Delhi, Bombay, Madras and Calcutta and Lucknow, Bangalore, Hyderabad, Chandigarh, Cuttack, Bhopal, Ahmedabad, Patna, Thiruvananthapuram, Jaipur and Jalandhar.

The number of Indian homes with TVs is estimated to be about 44 million by the end of 1994 and this is growing at the rate of 10 per cent annually.

Doordarshan, with its present network of 696 transmitting stations of various capacities. Thirty-two programme production centres and nearly 21,000 employees is one of the largest broadcasters in the world. Its signals cover 67.8 per cent of land area and are accessible to 85.1 per cent of the population, as on 1 January 1995. Out of a rural population of 627 million, 110 million viewers were hooked to Doordarshan.

The advertisement code of Doordarshan and All India Radio was amended in March, 1994 allowing advertisements relating to jewellery, precious stones, approved mutual funds, foreign banks including financial services, matrimonial agencies, astrologists, numerologists and manufacturers of hair-dye.

Cable Television (Regulation Bill)

About 75,000 operators are estimated to cater to 10 million homes wired by cable across the nation. The Government on 29 September 1994 promulgated the Cable Television (Regulation) Ordinance which was later passed as the Law, legitimizing the cable business and making the operators more accountable. The Bill made it mandatory for cable operators to be citizens of the country and restricted foreign equity in such networks to 49 per cent.

The Bill also provided for compulsory transmission of two Doordarshan satellite channels, and empowered the competent authority to prohibit transmission of certain programmes in the public interest. The Bill provided for registration of the existing cable operators within 90 days, and made the operation of non-registered cable networks an offence. It provided for the cable operators adhering to the prescribed programme and advertisement code and maintaining a register.

ANNEXURE III

PRESS COUNCIL GUIDELINES FOR REPORTING COMMUNAL INCIDENTS

The Press Council of India, while keeping in view that India is a country with a vastly diverse and differing range of languages, communities, regions and also with varying degree of economic prosperity suggested that the Press, in order to achieve national unity, should emphasise those aspects of the national life which underline the common features of diverse faiths and religions and subordination of sectional interests to national unity and integrity. The Council was, however, emphatic that the writings, which merely set forth or explain the grievances of a community, be it in any field social, political or economic and are meant to ventilate the grievances of a particular linguistic group of regions should not be considered communal. The Press Council laid down the following guidelines as offending against journalistic proprieties and ethics :

1. Distortion or exaggeration or facts or incidents in relation to communal matters or giving currency to univerified rumours, suspicions or inferences as if they were facts and base their comments on them.
2. Employment of intemperate or unrestrained language in the presentation of news or views, even as a piece of literary flourish or for the purpose of rhetoric or emphasis.
3. Encouraging or condoning violence even in the face of provocation as a means of obtaining redress of grievances whether the same be genuine or not.
4. While it is the legitimate function of the press to draw attention to the genuine and legitimate grievances of any community with a view to having the same redressed by all peaceful, legal and legitimate means, it is improper and a breach of journalistic ethics to invent griveances, or to exaggerate real grievances, as these tend to promote communal ill-feeling

and accentuate discord.

5. Scurrilous and untrue attacks on communities, or individuals, particularly when this is accompanied by charges, attributed misconduct to them, as due to their or of a particular community or caste.
6. Falsely giving a communal colour to incidents which might occur in which members of different communities happen to be involved.
7. Emphasising matters that are apt to produce communal hatred or ill-will, or fostering feelings of distrust between communities.
8. Publishing alarming news which are in substance untrue or make provocative comments on such news or even otherwise calculated to embitter relations between different communities or regional or linguistic groups.
9. Exaggerating actual happenings to achieve sensationalism and publication of news which adversely affect communal harmony with banner headlines or in distinctive types.
10. Making disrespectful, derogatory or insulting remarks on or reference to the different religions or faiths, or their founders.

ANNEXURE IV

SUGGESTED BASIC GUIDELINES FOR PROGRAMMING AND ADVERTISING CONTENT OF TRANSNATIONAL BROADCASTS

The Group was aware of the limitations imposed by the fact that legislation even if feasible would not succeed in serving the objective of ensuring respect for national sensitivities.

Moreover, film, television and other audio visual entertainment reflect the temper of each society, and uniformity of perceptions is not possible.

Therefore, the main responsibility of ensuring observance of principles should be on each country and its media organisations.

The suggestions appearing below have been formulated with a view to making transnational audio visual materials more acceptable and mutually beneficial. Most of these aspects are already contained in the broadcasting codes of almost all nations, but are sometimes rejected when transmitting broadcast material to other countries :

1. Expansion of intellectual horizons in social, economic, scientific, cultural and industrial fields with a view to enhancing global understanding and mutual prosperity.
2. Encouraging concepts of democracy, peace and cooperation as well as human values.
3. Avoiding the glorification of crime, violence and obscenity.
4. Recognising and projecting the family as the basic unit of society and inculcating a sense of love and dignity to embrace all ages and both sexes.
5. Promoting, with special care, the healthy development of children and youth as responsible and effective citizens of the future.
6. Creating an atmosphere of understanding, respect and tolerance towards all religions, cultures, languages, nationalities and ethnic groups and eschewing condescending attitudes based on ignorance, prejudice or mis-information.

7. Preserving general health and environment by discouraging hazardous products and habits.

A consensual approach to these guidelines could be promoted through regional and national broadcasting and advertising organisations. Since a large number of Radio and Television professionals are members of these organisations, their support could help change the media environment.

To achieve the objective, the following operational strategy is recommended :

(a) Involve apex bodies like Asian Broadcasting Union, Asia Pacific Broadcasting Union, SAARC, International Association of Advertisers, etc.

(b) Promote wider appreciation of the issues with the help of all the social and cultural organisations active in the region.

(c) Disseminate available research findings on social and economic impact of media and if adequate resources can be mobilised, undertake fresh research on the impact of transnational media on Asian Societies, especially on women and children.

(d) Communicate these guidelines to radio and television organisations, advertising associations, consumer movements, mass communication institutes, media critics, etc.

(e) Initiate suitable action through AMIC for a continuing dialogue with relevant organisations to secure their advice, commitment and assistance.

These guidelines were formulated at the Seminar on Legal and Regulatory Aspects of Satellite Broadcating held at New Delhi on 21-23 October, 1993, organised jointly by AMIC and the Broadcast Engineering Society of India.

ANNEXURE V

MONITORING MECHANISMS TO PROMOTE ETHICAL STANDARDS IN MEDIA

The AMIC and the Faculty of Communication Arts of Chulalongkom University jointly organised a three-day seminar on Media Monitors in Asia at Bangkok from 20 June to 1 July 1994. Among the conclusions that the seminar arrived at were recommendations on monitoring mechanisms to promote ethical standards in the media.

Statement of Recommendations

The Role of Media Monitoring Mechanisms in Promoting Ethical Standards : The multiplicity of media monitoring mechanisms at three levels are, namely: (a) statutory/official bodies, (b) trade organizations, and (c) public interest groups. It is recommended that media monitoring mechanisms should be democratic, representative and autonomous.

One of the functions of the media is to promote a competitive environment and thus prevent monopolistic tendencies by government and private enterprises. Whenever there is a possibility of conflict between media ownership and commercial interests, appropriate mechanisms should be put in place to ensure that media freedom does not suffer.

Media monitoring mechanisms should be continually updated and strengthened in terms of training, research and resource inputs with the view of upholding and promoting ethical standards.

Regional organizations should be encouraged to carry out comparative research on media ethics in the various countries of Asia. The output of such research should be widely publicized.

International linkages and information exchanges should be pursued among media monitoring bodies wherever possible. These activities should provide a basis for agreement on regionally acceptable ethical standards and for updating and strengthening capabilities for media monitoring.

Transnational producers in the media should be encouraged to follow regionally acceptable standards of ethics on issues such as violence, horror and sex.

Appropriate regional organizations should compile and circulate a recommended framework drawn from codes of ethics from various countries and invite communication practioners to define the framework in operational and actionable terms within their national contexts.

ANNEXURE VI

BROADCASTING CODE GOVERNING ALL INDIA RADIO

We recognize the immense power of Radio and Television for both good and evil and the solemn responsibilities this places upon all broadcasters.

We believe, there, that the following cardinal principles should be enshrined in the policy and practice of all Broadcasting and Television organizations :

- To ensure the objective presentation of news and fair and unbiased comment;
- To promote the advancement of education & culture;
- To raise and maintain high standards of decency and decorum in all programmes;
- To provide programmes for the young which, by variety and content, will inculcate the principles of good citizenship;
- To promote communal harmony, religious tolerance and international understanding;
- To treat controversial public issues in an impartial and dispassionate manner;
- To respect human rights and dignity.

(This Code was adopted by the Fourth Asian Broadcasters' Conference convened at Kuala Lumpur in 1962 and to which All India Radio was a party).

ANNEXURE VII

CODE OF ADVERTISING PRACTICE OF THE ADVERTISING STANDARDS COUNCIL OF INDIA

Chapter-I

To Ensure the Truthfulness and Honesty of Representations and Claims Made by Advertisements and to Safeguard against Misleading Advertisements

1. Advertisements must be truthful. All descriptions, claims and comparisons which relate to matters of objectively ascertainable fact should be capable of substantiation. Advertisers and advertising agencies are required to produce such substantiation as and when called upon to do so by The Advertising Standards Council of India.
2. Where advertising claims are expressly stated to be based on or supported by independent research or assessment, the source and date of this should be indicated in the advertisement.
3. Advertisements should not contain any reference to any person, firm or institution without due permission; nor should a picture of any generally identifiable person be used in advertising without due permission.
4. Advertisements shall not distort facts nor mislead the consumer by means of implications or omissions. Advertisements shall not contain statements or visual presentations which directly or by implication or by omission or by ambiguity or by exaggeration are likely to mislead the consumer about the product advertised or the advertiser or about any other product or advertiser.
5. Advertisements shall not be so framed as to abuse the trust of consumers or exploit their lack of experience or knowledge.

No advertisement shall be permitted to contain any claim so exaggerated as to lead to grave or widespread disappointment in the minds of consumers. For example :

(a) Products shall not be described as 'free' where there is any direct cost to the consumer other than the actual cost of any delivery, freight or postage. Where such costs are payable by the consumer a clear statement that this is the case shall be made in the advertisement.

(b) Where a claim is made that if one product is purchased another product will be provided 'free', the advertiser is required to show as and when called upon by The Advertising Standards Council of India that the price paid by the consumer for the product which is offered for purchase with the advertised incentive is no more than the prevalent price of the product without the advertised incentive.

(c) Claims which use expressions such as 'Up to five years' guarantee' or 'Prices from as low as Y' are not acceptable if there is a likelihood of the consumer being misled either as to the extent of the availability or as to the applicab:lity of the benefits offered.

(d) Special care and restraint has to be exercised in advertisements addressed to those suffering from weakness, any real or perceived inadequacy of any physical attributes such as height or bust development, obesity, illness, impotence, infertility, baldness and the like to ensure that claims or representations, directly or by implication, do not exceed what is considered prudent by generally accepted standards or medical practice and the actual efficacy of the product.

(e) Advertisements inviting the public to invest money shall not contain statements which may mislead the consumer in respect of the security offered, rates of return or terms of amortization; where any of the foregoing elements are contingent upon the continuance of or change in existing conditions, or any other assumptions, such conditions or assumptions must be clearly indicated in the advertisements.

(f) Advertisements inviting the public to take part in

lotteries or prize competitions permitted under the law or which hold out the prospects of gifts shall state clearly all material conditions so as to enable the consumers to obtain a true and fair view of their prospects in such activity. Further, such advertiser shall make adequate provisions for the judging of such competitions, announcement of the results and the fair distribution of prizes or gifts according to the advertised terms and conditions within a reasonable period of time. With regard to the announcement of results, it is clarified that the advertiser's responsibility under this section of the Code is discharged adequately if the advertiser publicizes the main result in the media used to announce the competition as far as is practicable, and advises the individual winners by post.

6. Obvious untruths or exaggerations intended to amuse or to catch the eye of the consumer are permissible, provided that they are clearly to be seen as humorous or hyperbolic and not likely to be understood as making literal or misleading claims for the advertised product.

Chapter-II

To Ensure that Advertisements are not Offensive to Generally Accepted Standards of Public Decency

Advertisements should contain nothing indecent, vulgar or repulsive which is likely, in the light of generally prevailing standards of decency and propriety, to cause grave or widespread offence.

Chapter-III

To Safeguard against the Indiscriminate Use of Advertising in Situations or for the Promotion of Products which are Regarded as Hazardous to Society or to Individuals to a degree or of a type which is Unacceptable to Society at Large

1. No advertisement shall be permitted which :

   (a) Tends to incite people to crime or to promote disorder and violence or intolerance.

   (b) Derides any race, caste, colour, creed or nationality.

(c) Presents criminality as desirable or directly or indirectly encourages people—particularly children—to emulate it or conveys the modus operandi of any crime.

(d) Adversely affects friendly relations with a foreign State.

2. Advertisements addressed to children shall not contain anything, whether in illustration or otherwise, which might result in their physical, mental or moral harm or which exploits their vulnerability. For example, no advertisement :

(a) Shall encourage children to enter strange places or to converse with strangers in an effort to collect coupons, wrappers, labels or the like.

(b) Should depict children leaning dangerously outside windows, over bridges or climbing dangerous cliffs and the like.

(c) Should show children climbing or reaching dangerously to reach products or for any other purpose.

(d) Should show children using or playing with matches or any inflammable or explosive substance; or playing with or using sharp knives, guns or mechanical or electrical appliances, the careless use of which could lead to their suffering cuts, burns, shocks or other injury.

(e) Shall feature minors for tobacco or alcohol based products.

3. Advertisements shall not, without justifiable reason, show or refer to dangerous practices or manifest a disregard for safety or encourage negligence.

4. Advertisements should contain nothing which is in breach of the law, or omit anything which the law requires.

5. Advertisements shall not propagate products, the use of which is banned under the law

Chapter-IV

To Ensure that Advertisements Observe Fairness in Competition such that the Consumer's Need to be Informed on Choices in the Market-place and the Canons of Generally Accepted Competitive Behaviour in Business are both Served

1. Advertisements containing comparisons with other manufacturers or suppliers or with other products, including those where a competitor is named, are permissible in the interests of vigorous competition and public enlightenment, provided :

   (a) It is clear what aspects of the advertiser's product are being compared with what aspects of the competitor's product.

   (b) The subject matter of comparison is not chosen in such a way as to confer an artificial advantage upon the advertiser or so as to suggest that a better bargain is offered than is truly the case.

   (c) The comparisons are factual, accurate and capable of substantiation.

   (d) There is no likelihood of the consumer being misled as a result of the comparison, whether about the product advertised or that with which it is compared.

   (e) The advertisement does not unfairly denigrate, attack or discredit other products, advertisers or advertisements directly or by implication.

2. Advertisements shall not make unjustifiable use of the name or initials of any other firm, company or institution, nor take unfair advantage of the goodwill attached to the trade mark or symbol of another firm or its product or the goodwill acquired by its advertising campaign.
3. Advertisements shall not be so similar to other advertisements in general layout, copy, slogans, visual presentations, music or sound effects as to be likely to mislead or confuse consumers.

BIBLIOGRAPHY

Acharya, R. N. (1987). *Television in India.* New Delhi : Manas Publications.

Agee, Warren K. (1969). *Mass Media in a Free Society.* New Delhi : Oxford and IBH Publishing Co.

Akash Bharati : National Broadcast Trust, Vol. 1. (1978)—Report of the Working Group on Autonomy for Akashvani and Doordarshan. New Delhi : Ministry of Information and Broadcasting.

AMIC (1985). *Satellite Technology : The Communication Equaliser.* Singapore.

An Indian Personality for TV, Vol. I. (1985). Report of the Working Group on Software for Doordarshan. New Delhi : Publications Division.

Anjana Maitra, Sinha (1993). *Women in a Changing Society.* New Delhi : Ashish Publishing House.

Arbind, K. Sinha (1987). *Mass Media and Rural Development : A Study of Village Communication in Bihar.* New Delhi : Concept Publishing Company.

Bahuguna, Sunder Lal (1994). Save Gangotri in Save Himalayas; Chipko Information Centre, Silyara, Tihri Garhwal, India, p. 20. *Ibid* : Development Redefined, p. 38.

Bhatt, Ela R. (1988). *Shramshakti.* New Delhi : National Commission on Self-Employed Women and Women in Informal Sector.

Bongartz, Heinz (1993). *Development Theories : NGOs and Self-Help Organizations.* Nepal Foundation for Advanced Studies, Kathmandu. p. 6.

Chawla, N. L. (1982). Communication Policy in India — Software Production and Distribution. *Communicator,* **XVII** (1) : 2-6, 10.

Chitnis, E. V. and Karnik, K. S. (1983). Technological Options Help us Get What we Seek. *Communicator,* **XVII** (3-4) : 24-28.

de Sola Pool, Ithiel (1980). The Governance of Broadcasting : Government, the Audience and Social Groups. In : *Development Digest* No. 2.

Dua, M. R. and Gupta, V. S. (eds.) (1994). *Media and Development.* New Delhi : Har Anand Publications.

Eapen, K. E. (ed.) (1989). *Role of Radio in Growth and Development.* Bangalore : Mass Media Education, Research and Information Centre.

Friedrich Ebert Stiftung, Bonn (1984). New Communication Technologies and their Impact on Western Industrialized Countries. *Communication Manual.*

Gerbner, George (1988). Violence and Terror in the Mass Media. Reports and Papers on Mass Communication. UNESCO.

Goonasekera. Anura (1993). Media Technology and Social Imperatives : An Examination of Communication Policies in Selected Asian Countries. *Media Asia,* **20** (4) : 194-204.

Guback, Thomas and Varis, Topio (1982). Transnational Communication and Cultural Industries. UNESCO.

Gupta, V. S. (1981). Communication Planning — A plea for appropriate communication. *Media Asia* **8** (3) : 156-161.

Gupta, V. S. and Ranjit Singh (1994). *Communication Planning for Socio-economic Development.* New Delhi : Har Anand Publications.

Gupta, V. S. (1995). *Third Revolution in Indian Perspective — Contemporary Issues and Themes in Communication.* New Delhi : Concept Publishing Company.

Joshi, P. C. (1986). *Communication and Nation Building : Perspective and Policy.* Sardar Patel Memorial Lectures (1995). New Delhi : Publications Division.

Khan, Rahat Nabi (1987). The Third Industrial Revolution : An Economic Overview. *Impact of Science on Society,* **146** : 115-122, UNESCO.

Kulandaiswamy, V. C. (1993). *Distance Education in the Indian Context.* IGNOU, New Delhi.

Lee, John A. R. (1976). *Towards Realistic Communication Policies.* Recent Trends and Ideas Compiled and Analysed. UNESCO.

Lerner, Daniel (1968). Modernisation : Social Aspects. *International Encyclopaedia of Social Sciences,* pp. 386-396. The Macmillan Company and The Press.

Luthra, H. R. (1986). Indian Broadcasting. New Delhi : Publications Division, Ministry of Information and Broadcasting, Govt. of India.

Masani, Mehra (1976). *Broadcasting and the People.* New Delhi : National Book Trust.

Mass Media in India (1993). New Delhi : Publications Division, Government of India.

Mathur, Kanwar, B. (1994). *Communication for Development and Social Change.* New Delhi : Allied Publishers.

Melkote, Srinivas R. (1991). *Communication for Development in the Third World - Theory and Practice.* New Delhi : Sage.

Menon, Narayana (1976). *The Communication Revolution.* New Delhi : National Book Trust. p. 86.

Michael Kunczik (1991). *Communication and Social Change.* Friedrich-Ebert-Stiftung, Bonn.

Ministry of Information and Broadcasting (1994-95). *Annual Report.* New

Delhi : Publications Division, Govt. of India.

Mitra, Anand (1993). *Television and Popular Culture in India*. New Delhi : Sage.

Mody, Bella (1984). Technology Option for Third World Countries : Do we have the freedom to choose. *Media Asia*, **11**(2) : 85-89.

Mowlana, Hamid and Laurie,-Wilson J. (1988). Communication Technology and Development. Reports and Papers on Mass Communication No. 101. UNESCO.

Nair, L. R. (1967). Private Press in National Development : The Indian Example. In : Lerner, Daniel and Wilbur Schramm (eds.) *Communication and Change in the Developing Countries*. Honolulu : East West Centre Press.

National Media Policy — A Discussion Paper. New Delhi : Ministry of Information and Broadcasting.

Rao, B. S. S. (1992). *Television for Rural Development*. New Delhi : Concept Publishing Company.

Sawant, B. P., Mohan, S. and Reddy B. P. Jeevan (1995). Supreme Court Judgement in Civil Appeals Nos. 1429-30 : Secretary, Ministry of Information and Broadcasting *vs* Cricket Association of Bengal.

Sayani, Ameen (1993). National and Transnational Censorship — Guidelines and Advertising Codes for Radio and Television. Paper presented at AMIC Seminar on the Legal and Regulatory Aspects of Satellite Broadcasting, New Delhi, 22-23 October.

Sayer, John (1987). Information Technology Contributes to Social Change in Asia. *Media Development*, **XXXIV** (4) : 7-9.

Shiva, Vandana (1992). *Women, Ecology and Health : Rebuilding Connections in Development Dialogue* (1-2). p. 3.

Singhal, Arvind and Rogers, Everett M. (1989). *India's Information Revolution*. New Delhi : Sage.

Srivastava, U. K. (1987). National Cost of Television in India in the Year 2000 — Socio-economic and Political Implications and Issues. *Media Asia*, **14** (3) : 136-148.

Thomas, P. N. (1993). Information and Change in India — Cultural Politics in a Post-modern Era. *Asian Journal of Communication*, **3** (1) : 64-83.

Tiwari., I. P. (1987). Communication, Technology and Development. New Delhi : Publications Division.

Toffler, Alvin (1975). *Future Shock*. London : Pan Books.

UNESCO (1982). *Many Voices, One World*. The International Commission on the Study of Communication Problems.

University Grants Commission — Countrywide Classroom — A Window on the World.

Venkateswaran, K. S. (1993). *Mass Media, Laws and Regulations in India.* AMIC.

Wang, Georgette (1991). Information Society in their Mind : A Survey of College Students in Seven Nations. *Asian Journal of Communication,* 1 (2) : 1-18.

Yadava, J. S. (1994). Communication and Development — The Indian Experience. In : Dua, M. R. and Gupta, V. S. (eds.), *Media and Development.* New Delhi : Har Anand Publications.

INDEX